# Working Water

ORO Editions
Publishers of Architecture, Art, and Design
Gordon Goff: Publisher

www.oroeditions.com
info@oroeditions.com

Published by ORO Editions



Book Design: Pablo Mandel
Text: Wenk Associates, Inc.
ORO Project Coordinator: Kirby Anderson

10 9 8 7 6 5 4 3 2 1 First Edition

Library of Congress data available upon request. World Rights: Available

ISBN: 978-1-943532-36-0

Color Separations and Printing: ORO Group Ltd.
Printed in China.

International Distribution: www.oroeditions.com/distribution

ORO Editions makes a continuous effort to minimize the overall carbon footprint of its publications. As part of this goal, ORO Editions, in association with Global ReLeaf, arranges to plant trees to replace those used in the manufacturing of the paper produced for its books. Global ReLeaf is an international campaign run by American Forests, one of the world's oldest nonprofit conservation organizations. Global ReLeaf is American Forests' education and action program that helps individuals, organizations, agencies, and corporations improve the local and global environment by planting and caring for trees.

# Working Water

## Reinventing the Storm Drain

WENK ASSOCIATES
PLANNERS AND LANDSCAPE ARCHITECTS

William E. Wenk, FASLA

ORO

ORO Editions — Novato, California

# Contents

# Introduction

## Water: Our Most Important Resource

Water is the source of life and the most important resource we have. Water has given form to and been a source of delight and inspiration in designed landscapes for thousands of years. Water defines the character of the land, especially in the semi-arid high plains environment of Denver, Colorado, where Wenk Associates' office resides. Exploring the potentials of urban water resources is an important part of the firm's practice, and has been throughout its thirty-seven-year history.

## Working Water

Working Water focuses on a select grouping of Wenk Associates' work that demonstrates how urban streams, rivers, and stormwater systems can be planned and designed to restore and enhance natural systems, adding value to communities. The projects range in scale from the design of a small rain garden at the firm's former office in Denver, to a revolutionary approach to managing stormwater and restoring the natural functions of the Los Angeles River. Most of the project examples explore the function of—and potential beauty in—the storm drain. They are at once pragmatic, detailed, and visionary in their approach to urban water resource management, presenting how stormwater, currently considered a waste, can instead be managed as a resource that adds value to the community and restores ecological function and health. *Working Water* reflects Wenk Associates' work from some of our earliest projects to our current ones. It is an assessment of how these projects have evolved and matured over time. It reveals successes—and failures—and considers new approaches for the future.

The book consists of three parts:

Part I describes the impacts of urbanization on the water cycle and the land. It explores how ancient and modern cultures managed available water resources differently, and explains how the best aspects of both water management systems can be integrated to address contemporary issues of water scarcity, improve water quality, and restore the natural functions of urban streams and rivers. This part also discusses how urban water resources can be better planned and designed to enhance natural systems and bring value to communities by, once again, creating places for people to gather.

Part II presents Wenk Associates' select projects that focus on working water. The projects range in scale and scope from small site design and stream corridor restoration to systems-planning for neighborhood districts and large river corridors.

Part III provides thoughts on the critical factors that have contributed to the success of Wenk Associates' built works, as well as lessons learned about legal, financial, and other challenges involved in designing and constructing landscapes to better manage water resources.

## Preface

# Inspired by Land and Water

The farm in southern Michigan.

In 1982, I founded Wenk Associates in Denver, Colorado, with a will to use landscape architecture to explore how to live well in the West. Given the scarcity of water and the dramatic growth in the region, a significant portion of our firm's practice focuses on how the design of water systems—specifically stormwater infrastructure and urban rivers and streams—can bring greater value to the natural function and livability of cities.

I grew up in southern Michigan on a small farm and graduated from high school believing I wanted to become a farmer. Those early years, shaped by the practicalities of working the land, formed my initial view of the landscape as a commodity. A large summer garden provided vegetables to feed us through the winter, and the farmhouse had two water systems—a well for drinking water and a cistern that stored rainwater from roof drains for bathing and washing. In the winter, our sawmill converted timber from local woodlots into lumber for local construction, and the "waste" that resulted from milling the timber provided fuel for heating our house and bedding for cattle.

As a teenager in the 1960s, the rapidly developing environmentalist movement introduced me to Stewart Udall's The Quiet Crisis, Rachel Carson's Silent Spring, and Aldo Leopold's Sand County Almanac. My old notion of "landscape as a commodity" evolved into a better awareness of environmental issues, and with that, a new appreciation of the landscape's intrinsic beauty and functional value as a natural system. This expanded interest in the land and ecological responsibility and a growing interest in art led me to take an introductory course in landscape architecture in college, where I began a new career path that would integrate my interests and my evolving landscape values.

My undergraduate studies in landscape architecture at Michigan State University gave me an excellent technical introduction to the profession and to designed landscapes. My studies introduced me to contemporary and historic landscape design precedents, but there was little discussion of land stewardship and how the profession could address growing concerns for environmental issues. I sought to reconcile my undergraduate education with my core values and the worldview that my upbringing had formed.

Shortly before completing my undergraduate degree, I read Ian McHarg's *De sign with Nature*. His critical connections between natural landscape processes and the planning and design professions encouraged me, as did Anne Wiston Spirn's *The Granite Garden*, a book that argues cities are a part of the natural world and should be designed to preserve and harness natural processes to make cities more livable. Upon graduation, these newfound principles provided a new universe of possibilities for me that more closely resembled my intuitive knowledge of, and commitment to, the landscape, forming the theoretical foundation for my life's work.

After three years of practice and nine months of travel across Europe and North Africa, I enrolled in a master's degree program in landscape architecture at the University of Oregon. There I developed an understanding of the importance of context and the intrinsic value of vernacular landscapes as I was introduced to more writers and thinkers, including J.B. Jackson, William Cronon, and Kenneth Helphand.

In the late 1960s, the Land Art movement began to unfold, suggesting how elements of traditional landscape design, design at the scale of the city, and the broader vernacular landscape could be integrated. The land art of Michael Heizer, especially his large earthworks like *Double Negative* (1969), inspired me, as did Walter De Maria's landscape installation *The Lightning Field.* The scale of these works reflects the qualities of the Western landscape, and their execution equals the directness of large public works projects.

Early in my career, I worked with civil engineers on a creek restoration project where I began to understand the potential value of urban infrastructure as a means to improve the livability and environmental qualities of our cities, and the critical role that civil engineers play in the design of stormwater systems. The need for and value of urban stormwater systems became obvious—stormwater systems have been fundamental to the development and growth of cities since antiquity. Unfortunately, the scale and shortsighted methods of city-building today contribute significantly to the declining quality of urban waterways and compromise the function of the natural water cycle. This understanding, and a desire to improve on the design of stormwater infrastructure, helped to form the foundation for Wenk Associates' work.

An underlying theme in the firm's professional practice is to "reinvent the storm drain." For me, this is a metaphor for expanding—down to the most basic details—the components of stormwater systems to invent new strategies for effective stormwater controls, and to promote the restoration of the natural functions of urban waterways in ways that add beauty and value to the urban landscape.

The projects described in this book have various influences. Some integrate the simplicity exemplified by the work of land artists and become a part of natural landscapes and processes, while others reflect more traditional landscape design principles. All the projects demonstrate aspects of working water, whether through practical and functional urban stormwater systems or urban stream rehabilitation. Our project examples mediate between the large-scale industrial qualities of contemporary single-purpose stormwater systems and the preindustrial, more humanly scaled, ways of living on the land that are well crafted, integrating function and beauty and a respect for context.

The environmental crises we face today—especially climate change and shrinking supplies of clean water—require us to rethink the most basic components of traditional urban systems and to identify a broader toolkit for a more resilient approach to city-building. There has been progress. The "big moves"—large, individual, public works projects—have transformed how communities view waterways and have redefined the value of urban waterways and urban stormwater. Small-scale incremental implementation of green infrastructure, such as green roofs, stormwater gardens, or porous pavement can be effective at improving water quality. This piecemeal approach—even if large- and small-scale projects are combined—is not enough to meet the national goal of making urban waterways fishable and swimmable. We must expand our approach to implement systems that integrate individual sites and projects to exert greater influence over our common public landscapes and the infrastructure frameworks of the city. We must develop new components that can supplement or replace conventional stormwater systems with natural technologies and adapt this essential city infrastructure to sustain the natural world that we rely on for our existence.

Wenk Associates' practice seeks to challenge our clients, partners, and cities to identify and institute new green infrastructure methods not only at the site scale, but at the district and community scale, as an updated standard of practice for stormwater-system design in our cities. This book has evolved as a reflection on over thirty years of our professional work. It is a monograph describing selected projects of the firm that focus on urban water resources. It is a teaching tool for students and the interested public and public officials that wish to explore new ways of managing urban-water resources. It is also a vision for the future.

It is my hope that by sharing our firm's work and the valuable lessons we have learned, we will inform the next generation of stormwater infrastructure, resulting in healthier urban and natural systems that make our cities better places in which to live.

Bill Wenk, FASLA
*Spring 2021*

*Double Negative,* Clark, Nevada by Michael Heizer.
Photo Credit: Ken McCown, 2012

Below: Storm drain, ancient Rome. Traditional stormwater systems have supported the development of cities since ancient times.

Right: My travels through North Africa in a camper van in the winter of 1973 broadened my view of the world and the landscape. I took an early morning walk at the edge of the Sahara Desert in northern Algeria and happened upon this scene. The ability of this farmer to subtly manipulate a hostile landscape by using "natural technologies" to create a productive garden of onions and date palms had a profound influence on my career. His use of the site's context also demonstrates the essence and beauty of formal garden design.

Part I

# Land, Water, and Resilient Communities

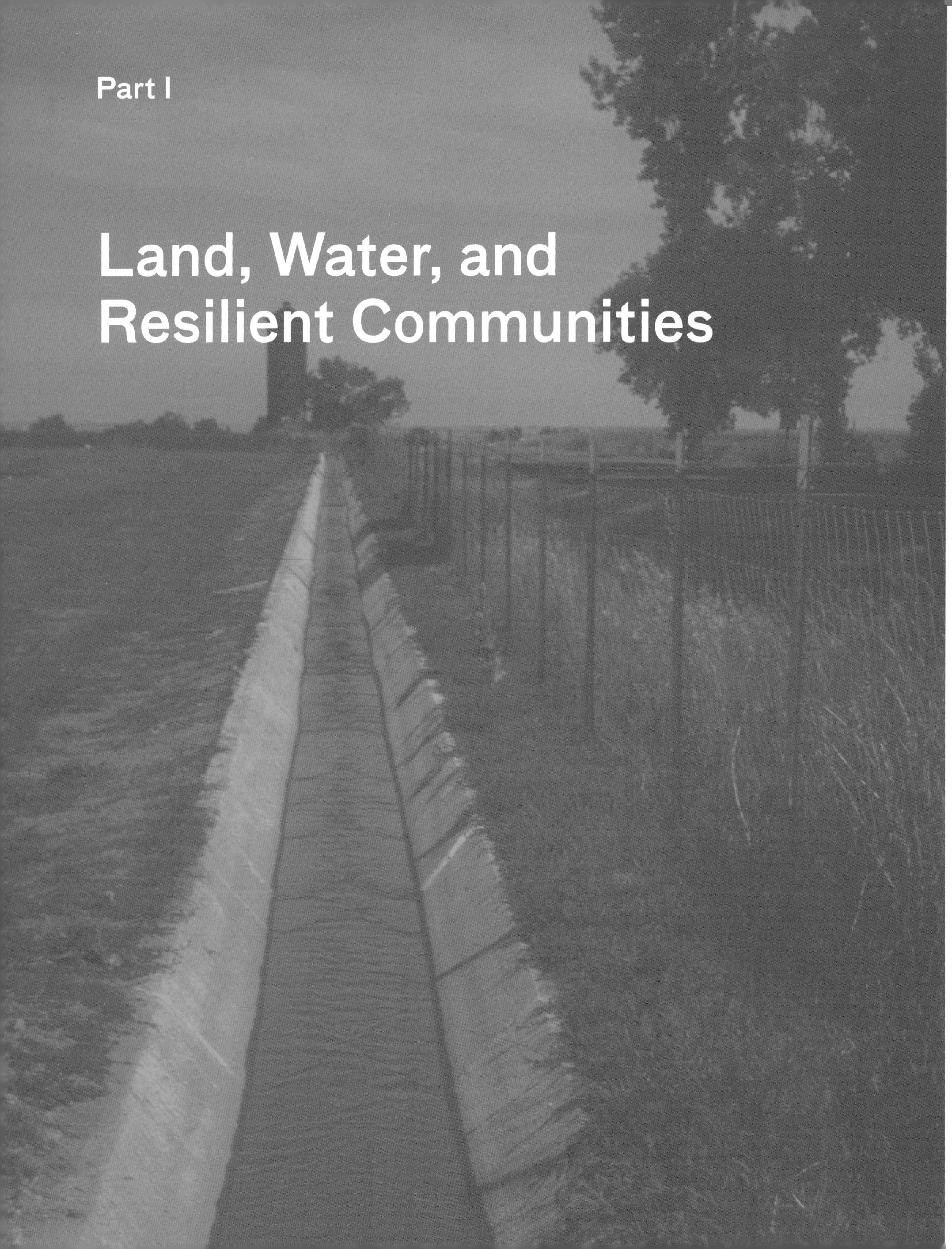

## Water as a Resource

Water resource management ties closely to culture and technology. More advanced pre-industrial cultures developed highly specialized cities with sophisticated urban infrastructure. This infrastructure supported large populations that often exceeded the carrying capacity of locally available resources, including water supplies. These systems typically relied on the ingenious use of local materials and natural systems and processes— "natural technologies"—which allowed cities to grow beyond the carrying capacity of the surrounding landscape.

The advent of the industrial era in the nineteenth century changed everything. The rapid growth and industrialization of modern cities led to the development of separate water supply and disposal systems. City builders abandoned the natural technologies that were so important for pre-industrial cities, in favor of vastly more complex technological systems. These new systems were often large-scale and dependent on distant power sources, using involved mechanical systems and chemical treatment processes. Pumps enabled drinking water supplies to be transported through pipes over great distances or from deep wells, which eliminated a city's dependency on natural technologies for water supply or waste disposal. Nearby rivers and streams, once seen as essential to survival, became polluted dumping grounds.

Rainfall, once carefully collected and stored, was now treated as waste—a hazard to be feared and a source of disease that should be disposed of—rather than as a resource that could be managed and integrated back into the community. The primary goal of modern stormwater systems evolved to quickly convey and dispose of rainfall into nearby rivers and streams. The scale of large industrial cities led to concentrations of contaminants and changes in river hydrology that transformed urban streams into engineered extensions of the city's disposal systems, often with concrete channels or underground piping, which eliminated the purifying effects of rainfall flowing to waterways through natural systems.

In most cities today, vast networks of subsurface piped stormwater disposal systems have erased minor streams from the urban landscape. Concentrated flows of these now-buried natural streams, along with large volumes of rainfall, discharge from pipes into waterways as part of the city's disposal system. Along the way, these flows collect trash, animal waste, fertilizers and pesticides, and other pollutants from lawns, streets, and parking lots—virtually every surface in the city—and discharge it all directly into rivers and streams. This is known as non-point source pollution. In many older cities, raw sewage is also collected by the same system of pipes as stormwater and during periods of heavy rainfall is also discharged directly into rivers and streams. These events are known as combined sewer overflows or CSOs. Today, most urban streams in our country contain levels of pollutants that, generally, make their water unsafe for swimming and human consumption without extensive treatment and that deplete their natural value. Non-point source pollution degrades the natural water cycle of once healthy watersheds to the extent that streams no longer have the potential to naturally cleanse and restore themselves.

The Hydrologic Cycle on Undisturbed Land

1. Water vapor rises due to evaporation from water bodies and transpiration from vegetation.
2. Water vapor condenses and falls to earth as rainfall.
3. Vegetation transpires water vapor and temporarily stores rainfall before infiltration into the soil as groundwater.
4. Rainfall from large storms and groundwater that supports the flow of waterways sustain rivers and streams in a natural state. Temporary storage and infiltration of excess runoff in wetlands and stream sinuosity slow the rate of runoff and supplement groundwater recharge.

## The Hydrologic Cycle

The development of watersheds over time is a result of the hydrologic cycle. When undisturbed, watersheds evolve in a state of dynamic stability through processes of erosion, deposition of sediments, and changes to the landscape to create a rich mosaic of streams and rivers, land masses, and plant and animal communities. The study of the movement of water across the landscape is known as the hydrology of a river, stream, or watershed. Hydraulics describe the physical actions of the movement of water through streams and rivers. A designer's basic understanding of the hydrologic cycle and hydrology, principles of stream hydraulics, and the impacts of urbanization and other land disturbances on stream hydrology is beneficial for productive collaboration with engineers, hydrologists, ecologists, and others on the restoration of streams and rivers and the design of stormwater systems.

The water cycle provides a supply of clean, fresh water through processes of evaporation, condensation, precipitation, infiltration, surface runoff, and subsurface flow to streams, rivers, lakes, and groundwater, and sustains all natural systems on Earth. Undisturbed vegetation—especially native forests, grasslands, and porous native soils—typically slows down storm runoff, allowing most of it to infiltrate into the soil during most rainfall events. Only the largest storms generate surface runoff. During a typical rain event on undisturbed land, rainfall moves below the surface of the ground as groundwater then enters rivers and streams and recharges aquifers as an ongoing supply of clean, fresh water. Rivers and streams in their native form typically meander, and groundwater and storm runoff support a diversity of plant communities that further cleanse water of contaminants. The natural meander of streams and rivers and

floods that pond in shallow depressions allows storm runoff to infiltrate to resupply groundwater aquifers and support riparian plant communities.

There is a finite amount of fresh water on Earth; however, intense urbanization presents widespread negative effects on the ability of the water cycle to cleanse water through natural processes. An awareness of how urban development changes the land and affects the water cycle is important in understanding how the design of contemporary stormwater systems could be modified to better support natural processes.

## The Effects of Urbanization and Other Land Modifications

Urban development, cultivation, or other significant changes to the land on simply a small portion of a watershed disrupts the watershed's natural hydrology and stream hydraulics, typically destabilizing waterways and causing excessive erosion. Waterway destabilization tends to occur in the following sequence: 1) land use and land cover are altered, as vegetation and topsoil are removed to make way for agriculture, buildings, roads, and other urban infrastructure; and 2) these changes and the introduction of a constructed drainage network then alter the local hydrology so that streams and rivers receiving runoff experience radically different rates and amounts of runoff, or flow regimes. Nearly all the problems associated with destabilized waterways result from one underlying cause—the loss of the soil and the vegetation's ability to retain water and transfer water to the atmosphere by evaporation.

In undeveloped areas, rainfall typically infiltrates into the soil or is evapotranspired by vegetation. In cities these processes are diminished, so stormwater flows rapidly across the altered land surface and arrives at the stream channel in short, concentrated

**The Hydrologic Cycle on Disturbed Land**

1. Water vapor rises due to evaporation from water bodies and transpiration from vegetation.
2. Water vapor condenses and falls to earth as rainfall.
3. Buildings, roads, and other impervious surfaces prevent infiltration of rainfall. Rainfall flows on the surface, carrying contaminants along streets and through underground pipes rapidly and directly to the river, causing surges in the river flow which causes erosion and other disruptions to its natural state.
4. Urbanization typically results in filling in river valleys, straightening channels, and reducing vegetation, which further degrades the river's ability to sustain natural processes.

bursts of high-volume discharge. When combined with nonpoint source pollutants from lawns, motor vehicles, domestic animals, industry, and other sources, these hydrologic changes and pollutants erode streambanks and degrade water quality and wildlife habitat in virtually all urban streams (taken, in part, from *Urban Stormwater Management in the United States*, National Research Council, the National Academies Press, Summary, p5).

Pre-industrial settlements had a more limited impact on watersheds. Cities were smaller, and water supply and disposal systems were often dependent on the storage and reuse of rainfall, which reduced the impact of storm runoff on nearby streams.

## Ancient to Modern Ways with Water

Machu Picchu, the royal estate of the Inca ruler Pachacuti, is one of the best-known and most spectacular archaeological sites in the world. Built in the mountains of Peru, Machu Picchu was occupied from 1450 to 1572 A.D., when it was abandoned with the collapse of the Incan Empire. Incan cities such as Machu Picchu represent a triumph of site planning and design, enduring craftsmanship, and sophisticated engineering.

Machu Picchu's spring-fed canal and fountains were part of a water system that was both functional and beautiful. It provided drinking water for the people who lived there, irrigation water for an extensive agricultural area, and stormwater drainage to support the city. In public places, people gathered near the water for practical reasons, to obtain drinking water or to wash clothes, and for recreation and respite. The archeological site endures today only because its sophisticated design, construction, and water supply and drainage systems were rooted in natural technologies.

During the twentieth century in the United States, the rapid growth of industrial cities resulted in the development of technological water systems that largely abandoned multifunctional pre-industrial water systems like those at Machu Picchu and other Incan cities.

Mechanization encouraged the development of standard components for stormwater systems and other infrastructure that could be easily and quickly replicated in almost any environment to accommodate the expansive new industrial centers that were developing. McMillan Reservoir in Washington, D.C., however, is a notable exception.

McMillan Reservoir Park, a nearly forgotten twenty-five acres in northeast Washington, D.C., is an example of a water system that combined elements of typical contemporary systems with pre-industrial multifunctional systems like those found at Machu Picchu. McMillan Reservoir, beginning at the turn of the nineteenth century supplied much of the city's drinking water, which was fed by gravity into twenty sand-filled underground vaults that filtered out impurities. A deck above the vaults featured a formal park, green with plants, that was designed in 1904 by Frederick Law Olmsted, Jr., a renowned founder of the profession of landscape architecture. Even the aboveground sand storage towers at this reservoir were stunning examples of industrial design.

The reservoir and park, used for recreation until 1941, closed when, with the advent of World War II, public officials became concerned that saboteurs would poison the water. In the 1980s, the sand filtration plant itself was retired. Since then, various redevelopment schemes failed, and today the site remains empty and fenced-off. Yet even as an urban ruin, McMillan Reservoir continues to be an excellent example of how the resourcefulness of ancient systems can be integrated with contemporary stormwater systems, providing essential water functions, vital public infrastructure, and civic value (reference *Ecology and Design*, Chapter 7: "Toward an Inclusive Concept of Infrastructure," William E. Wenk, p173–175, ed. Bart Johnson and Kristina Hill, Island Press).

Left: Sand filtration towers along a pedestrian promenade at McMillan Reservoir in Washington, D.C., decommissioned and closed in 1941. Photo credit: Brit Flicks, June 2014, Courtesy of Friends of McMillan Park

Below: Water infrastructure at Tipón, an Inca ruin near Cusco, Peru. Photo credit: Ruth Wright

## Natural Technologies

"Natural technologies" are tools, systems, or processes that are the result of adapting, employing, or otherwise using the natural resource for human use without degrading that resource. Natural technologies favor a more benevolent shaping of the land. Natural technologies make use of natural processes, such as water flow or sand filtration, to conserve and use water resources for multiple benefits. Built water systems work more efficiently with natural flows and processes, and when properly applied, natural technologies can create a managed ecological landscape that provides high-quality human habitats while minimizing impacts on natural ecosystems.

The concept of natural technologies has deep historical roots, much deeper than the McMillan Reservoir or even Machu Picchu. In what is now metropolitan Phoenix, the Hohokam built 1,250 miles of gravity-fed irrigation canals across the Salt River Valley. They recycled water in and out of the river, rather than damming and depleting this basic resource. Their systems lasted more than 1,500 years (from about 100 B.C. to 1450 A.D.), and later became the basis for the ditch irrigation systems still used in Arizona.

Gravity-fed systems of irrigation ditches and canals are still prevalent throughout the arid American West. Water diverted from the Rocky Mountains' distant watersheds across the Continental Divide nourishes the historic High Line Canal that meanders through Denver. The canal corridor is a linear park teeming with wildlife and shaded by huge cottonwoods, a seventy-one-mile ribbon of green, enjoyed daily by walkers and bikers as they wind through city and county jurisdictions. The infrastructure of the High Line's water-delivery system creates an integrated landscape with places for habitat and recreation. After more than 100 years of use, the city plans to repurpose portions of the High Line Canal that have been abandoned to make them a part of the city's stormwater management system, thus improving the quality of urban runoff and continuing to sustain the trees that line the canal.

## Industrialization and Rethinking Standardized Stormwater Systems

The Industrial Revolution and seemingly limitless land and resources fueled the explosive growth of American cities in the nineteenth century. There was little or no concern for the destruction of entire landscapes to fuel growth, and the stormwater systems of cities often combined raw sewage and industrial wastes with stormwater in one sewer system (commonly known as combined sewers), to maximize their efficiency. Urban waterways became so polluted that they were unfit for any use.

In the early 1970s, Congress passed the Clean Water Act, which required separation and treatment of discharges from combined sewers, typically referred to as "point-source discharges." As a result, most cities made significant progress in eliminating overflows from combined sewers, and greatly reduced the discharge of industrial wastes and raw sewage. The quality of most urban waterways improved significantly.

Modern stormwater systems improved in other ways. Stormwater system piping, culverts, inlets, and outfalls are now standardized components included in design manuals issued by cities and public agencies across the country, resulting in greater efficiencies in system design and construction. The development of sophisticated planning models that more accurately predict flooding allows cities to better manage flood risk. Numerical standards such as the "100-year flood event" are useful in that they define a generally accepted level of risk for development. Federal standards for measuring nonpoint source pollutants, or pollution from many diffuse sources such as runoff, precipitation, drainage, seepage, and hydrologic modification, base their effectiveness on achieving reductions in numerical values (parts per million, for example) for a given contaminant. A recent National Science Foundation study, however, determined that a reduction in flow rate—typically achieved using natural technologies such as green infrastructure—is more effective and is a more meaningful measurement of the reduction in pollutant levels.

Although improved regulations typically require the separation of combined sewers, and technical efficiencies greatly improve the performance of modern stormwater systems, nonpoint source pollution is increasing in most urban streams and rivers. Stormwater is still disposed of as waste, so urban waterways are almost universally unfit for swimming and many have greatly reduced ecological function and value be-

High Line Canal, Arapahoe County, Colorado.
Photo credit: Denver Water

cause of nonpoint source pollution. Extreme flood events, because of global warming, present an especially urgent challenge.

Standard green infrastructure practices such as biofiltration swales, stormwater gardens, and other low-impact development (LID) techniques are implemented widely, although poor construction and maintenance practices often limit their effectiveness. Piecemeal implementation of green infrastructure that is the norm today has little chance of improving the health of urban streams and rivers or better protecting against increased flooding. Modern engineered stormwater systems, when supplemented with natural technologies and implemented at the scale of a small watershed, neighborhood, or district, hold more potential for restoring the health of urban waterways and mitigating the impacts of flooding. Stormwater brings added value when it is managed to supplement urban water supply and used as a recreational resource rather than being disposed of as waste.

The challenges of flood risk, scarce water supplies, and damage to the natural qualities of urban streams and rivers have never been greater. The levels of pollution continue to rise and financial resources to address those issues have never been more limited. It is time for a bolder approach, with new and expanded ways of managing urban stormwater resources.

## Designing the Next Generation of Green Infrastructure

Whether cities can retrofit stormwater systems with green infrastructure at a scale that results in significant reduction in levels of contamination remains to be seen, given their limited scale and fragmented and piecemeal implementation. This is especially true in existing cities where opportunities for implementation are severely limited.

The next generation of green infrastructure must be at a district or community scale, and must combine the best features of contemporary stormwater systems and ancient systems that are based on natural technologies. The tool kit of green infrastructure best practices, including biofiltration and swales that have become standard practice, can be expanded to supplement or replace other standard components of contemporary stormwater systems to mimic and restore the original hydrology of urban watersheds.

To understand how these contemporary stormwater systems might work, we should look carefully at the contemporary vernacular regional landscape. Understanding how the technologies used to manage water resources in the past can inform more resilient development patterns for the future.

The High Plains of Colorado.

Opposite: Traditional irrigation systems domesticated the prairie, creating a productive landscape that integrates rural and natural qualities.

## Land and Natural Technologies

Civilizations have colonized and thrived in inhospitable landscapes for thousands of years by using ingenuity and the resources at hand. The settlement potential of the High Plains of Colorado, a harsh and unforgiving landscape at the foot of the Rocky Mountains, is possible only because of the extensive diversion and distribution of local and distant water supplies. Without the ingenious manipulation of watersheds, extensive settlement would not be possible.

The environmental costs of large-scale water diversions are significant. Alternatives for wise water management present themselves when we study successful traditional irrigation methods and understand how they can be adapted to allow a wiser use of urban water resources. Careful observation of traditional irrigation systems inspired the approaches to many of the projects described in Part 2 of this book.

### The Colorado Prairie: A Place of Extremes without Scale

The semi-arid prairie of the High Plains along the Front Range of the Colorado Rocky Mountains is a place of extremes, where the lack of water, rapid swings in temperature, and vast open spaces define a landscape where the horizon extends forever. In contrast to the forests, lakes, fields, and settlements of more temperate climates, the native prairie, where earth meets sky, is a powerful place that is sublime in its vastness. It is a landscape where human scale is measured against the vast scale of the prairie.

The wind always blows on the open prairie, and it is either too hot or too cold. Distances are deceptive, as landmarks that appear to be near might be miles away. Water is scarce, averaging fourteen to fifteen inches a year, even along streambeds that are typically dry until it rains. Rain and snow often come as violent storms, dramatic expressions of nature's power. The only way to live comfortably on this semi-arid landscape is in "oases"—settlements that have a source of water, provide protection from the elements, and create a sense of place.

### The Domestication of the Prairie Using Traditional Irrigation Practices

The prairie becomes more familiar when it is transformed by settlement. Fields, fences, farmsteads, and towns give it a human scale and identity. Any significant prairie settlement is possible only because of an extensive infrastructure of water diversion, collection, storage, and redistribution, often drawn from distant watersheds. On the Front Range, water delivery to the prairie typically requires water to be transported in tunnels through the Continental Divide, then stored in reservoirs. From there, the vast gravity-fed irrigation network of diversions, canals and ditches, head gates, and furrows delivers water to farms, ranches, fields, and pastures. Water for these landscapes often creates highly productive and ecologically diverse rural places of great beauty.

## Adapting Natural Technologies to Address Urban Stormwater Challenges

Disruption of the natural hydrologic cycle due to urbanization or other disturbances in a watershed presents multiple challenges. A watershed's original hydrology, or predevelopment hydrology, derives from the infiltration of rainfall and its slow release as groundwater to rivers and streams. In contrast, traditional urban stormwater systems convey rainfall directly into rivers and streams, carrying with it contaminants, and create extreme fluctuations in flow that damage the original natural qualities of downstream rivers and streams.

To restore a watershed's original function, water must be absorbed into the soil, filtered, and released slowly to return to the river and continue the water cycle. Traditional agricultural irrigation systems and conventional stormwater systems share much in common, with one important difference. Traditional irrigation systems collect, convey, store, and then redistribute collected water as a valuable resource to irrigate agricultural lands; while conventional urban stormwater systems collect, convey, store, and dispose of rainfall as waste. Contemporary green infrastructure stormwater systems can integrate some of the best qualities of traditional agricultural irrigation into conventional stormwater systems. The large scale of agricultural systems and the efficient means by which they collect, store, and transport water and widely disperse it across and infiltrate it into the landscape provide valuable precedents for planners and designers.

In other words, dispersed urban rainfall can grow natural areas (and in the process remove contaminants) as effectively as dispersed irrigation flows can grow crops.

## Global Implications for Stormwater Management

Colorado cities share many of the same challenges as most cities nationally and globally. Global warming has affected the hydrological cycle—coastal cities are more susceptible to hurricanes and rainfall patterns are changing globally. Most cities are experiencing storms of greater intensity and duration, some with more total rainfall, some with much less. In some areas it is not uncommon to hear of rivers that "never" flood to experience multiple 100-year or even 500-year flood events in a short period of time.

Although many regions enjoy more abundant water resources than the semi-arid west, many cities still depend on rivers and streams, lakes, and groundwater sources for their water supply which present health risks requiring expensive and elaborate water treatment in order for it to be safe for drinking. Cities in all climates share these risks associated with increased flooding.

In most ways, solutions to scarcity, contamination, flood events, and other challenges to any city's water supply and urban stormwater management can be addressed, in part, by changing how we manage our urban water resources as part of systems that employ the widespread use of natural technologies.

Top: **Collect–Convey–Store–Disperse**
Traditional agricultural irrigation system.

Bottom: **Collect–Convey–Dispose**
Conventional stormwater system.

Right: **Collect–Convey–Disperse**
Contemporary integrated stormwater system.

## Rethinking Stormwater Management in Today's Cities

The need for new sources of clean fresh water has never been greater. Water supplies that support the millions of people living in cities and towns in the Rocky Mountain region, especially in the Front Range urban corridor along the eastern edge of the Rocky Mountains, cannot be met by supplies that are currently available. Colorado's Department of Local Affairs (DOLA, 2015) projects the state's population to nearly double to 8.6 to 10 million people by 2050, which per Colorado's Water Plan (State of Colorado 2015) will create a need for an additional six hundred thousand to one million acre-feet of water annually to meet future demands. Some areas of the state (e.g., the South Denver metro area) already need to replace nontributary groundwater supplies; therefore, simply acquiring new supplies within the state to meet future needs is not an option.

Traditional agricultural irrigation practices that collect, store, and distribute stormwater can inspire new types of contemporary urban stormwater systems that combine the best of gray, conventional subsurface piped systems, and green, stormwater systems based on natural technologies, to manage stormwater as a resource.

Legal, financial, and institutional barriers in Colorado and elsewhere limit or prohibit many uses of stormwater and often discourage more robust stormwater systems that use stormwater as a resource. However, a more multifunctional approach holds great promise as a means of expanding the tool kit of standard details of contemporary stormwater systems to restore natural stream functions, reduce demands on potable water supplies, improve the quality of urban runoff, and to realize the potential of urban stormwater resources for making cities better places to live.

The piecemeal implementation of green infrastructure is not enough to address the issues of poor watershed health and the quality of urban runoff. Conventional stormwater systems contribute significantly to those problems and to other impacts on urban rivers and streams. A broader array of standard stormwater system details that modify and expand urban stormwater systems making them more environmentally responsible and valuable as civic amenities is needed. Standard stormwater system transformation is essential for the health of urban rivers and streams and the availability of clean fresh water for all. Part 2 of this book describes a series of projects that illustrate an array of approaches to working water, implemented at a variety of scales and through different project types, which enhance the natural potential and civic value of urban stormwater systems.

**Collect – Convey – Dispose**
Traditional gray stormwater infrastructure.

Above: A conventional gray stormwater outfall discharges and disposes of contaminated stormwater directly into the creek.

Right: The stormwater outfall and trickle channel pans of this neighborhood detention pond limit use of the detention pond for recreational use, open space, or for water quality treatment. Photo credit: Barr Engineering Company

**Collect—Convey—Disperse**
Green technologies replace traditional gray stormwater infrastructure.

Stormwater level spreaders disperse and infiltrate rather than discharge and dispose of contaminated stormwater. Spreaders, which can take on many forms, evenly distribute flows mimicking the function of traditional agricultural irrigation systems and the hydrologic cycle. These examples illustrate standard details found in the Denver region's Mile High Flood District *Urban Storm Drainage Criteria Manual, Volume 3* as standard stormwater Best Management Practices.

Above: Level spreader – Aurora Sports Park, Aurora, Colorado.

Left: Level spreader – Heritage Park Development, Minneapolis, Minnesota. Photo credit: Barr Engineering Company

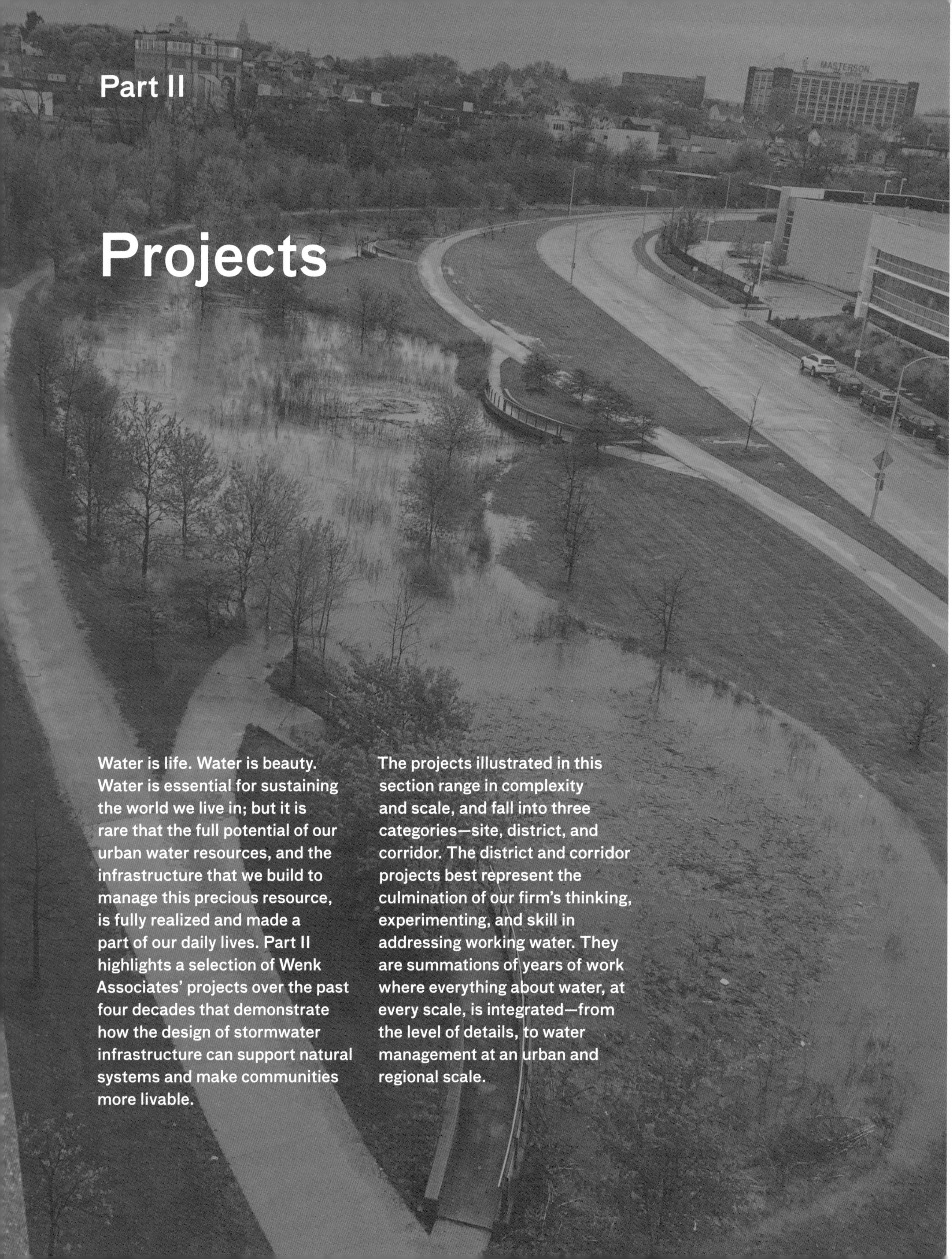


# Part II

# Projects

Water is life. Water is beauty. Water is essential for sustaining the world we live in; but it is rare that the full potential of our urban water resources, and the infrastructure that we build to manage this precious resource, is fully realized and made a part of our daily lives. Part II highlights a selection of Wenk Associates' projects over the past four decades that demonstrate how the design of stormwater infrastructure can support natural systems and make communities more livable.

The projects illustrated in this section range in complexity and scale, and fall into three categories—site, district, and corridor. The district and corridor projects best represent the culmination of our firm's thinking, experimenting, and skill in addressing working water. They are summations of years of work where everything about water, at every scale, is integrated—from the level of details, to water management at an urban and regional scale.

**SITE-SCALE** projects are site specific, with definite goals and well-defined improvements for the project area that, for the most part, have been carried through design and construction. We have had the benefit of watching several of these built projects mature over a number of years, allowing us to study and learn from their progress, including the stormwater gardens at our former office and the restoration of Shop Creek in Aurora, Colorado.

**DISTRICT-SCALE** projects typically encompass larger areas or neighborhoods with multiple ownerships, on both public and private lands. Plans are often implemented through multiple phases by both the public and private sectors. For example, our work to revitalize the Menomonee River Valley in Milwaukee spanned a decade and involved numerous public and private development partners to develop a series of increasingly refined master plans that were implemented in multiple phases. The work included construction of site infrastructure, landscape restoration, and park development, as well as private infill development projects.

**CORRIDOR PROJECTS**, specifically river corridor projects, share similarities with district-scale projects, but are often more complex. This type of project typically cuts across multiple districts or neighborhoods and often includes miles of urban waterways that require highly specialized hydraulic and hydrologic engineering, permitting by multiple local and federal agencies, and water quality and wildlife habitat improvements. For example, the master plan vision for the Los Angeles River dictates the reconstruction of natural river functions, riverfront revitalization in multiple neighborhoods, new and enhanced parks, and a more resilient stormwater infrastructure to improve water quality and restore aquatic and riparian habitats.

Part II features projects located in urban, suburban, and mountain settings, from rural prairie landscapes to derelict urban industrial sites in cities in the West and Midwest. Many of the project sites had significant environmental challenges, including contamination from mining or past industrial use and stream degradation due to urbanization. Several focus on the adaptive reuse of existing infrastructure as land uses changed over time or as the infrastructure no longer met community needs.

Although these select projects vary greatly in scale, type, and complexity, their primary goals were the same:

1) to manage urban stormwater, and 2) to design landscapes that support healthy natural systems and add value by creating places for people. These projects offer case studies for urban stormwater infrastructure and urban waterway solutions, and demonstrate how our cities can become more resilient, and ultimately, better places to live.

# Wenk Office Stormwater Gardens

Denver, Colorado

**The gardens were a manifestation of the firm's philosophy on the wise use of water in the West.**

In 1998, Wenk Associates purchased a vacant commercial building for the firm's growing practice. The move provided an opportunity to test new ways of designing stormwater gardens as part of renovating the building site. The use of contemporary urban garden forms and readily available materials used in modern flood irrigation systems served as a garden framework. The gardens became a place for informal gathering for staff in a setting appropriate to the region and to the building's urban context.

Located in a transitional neighborhood near downtown Denver, the one-story commercial building lacked curb appeal, and the surrounding landscape was mostly paved. As part of a comprehensive renovation of the building, and because of its limited quarter-acre site, an unnecessary driveway was removed and replaced with three stormwater gardens inspired by traditional Colorado agricultural irrigation techniques used along the Front Range of the Rocky Mountains. Instead of using irrigation water stored in reservoirs, stormwater from three of the building's four downspouts sustained three of the gardens. Natural rainfall, with occasional supplemental irrigation, sustained a fourth dryland garden.

The gardens represented native and cultured landscapes, each responsive to the amount of water available and to its varied context. Native riparian sedges and rushes planted as part of the splash gardens at downspouts thrived through periodic inundation and extended drought with no maintenance. The driest gardens, planted with xeric groundcovers and prairie grasses, were sustained only by natural rainfall and occasional flood irrigation. More refined, maintenance-intensive xeric gardens near the building entrance and interior public areas provided shade for an employee patio and a viewing garden that was a richly patterned floral mosaic of xeric groundcovers.

In 2004, Wenk Associates moved to a new location and the gardens were removed when the site was redeveloped.

Right: Grids of surface channels and subsurface PVC pipe mimic traditional agricultural irrigation techniques and direct runoff to irrigate the gardens.

Opposite, top & lower left: The building and site before and after renovation.

Opposite, lower right: The viewing garden incorporates low walls to control the splash from overhead downspouts and informal seating. Splash gardens are planted with sedges and rushes and flood-irrigated gardens with xeric grasses, groundcovers, and succulents.

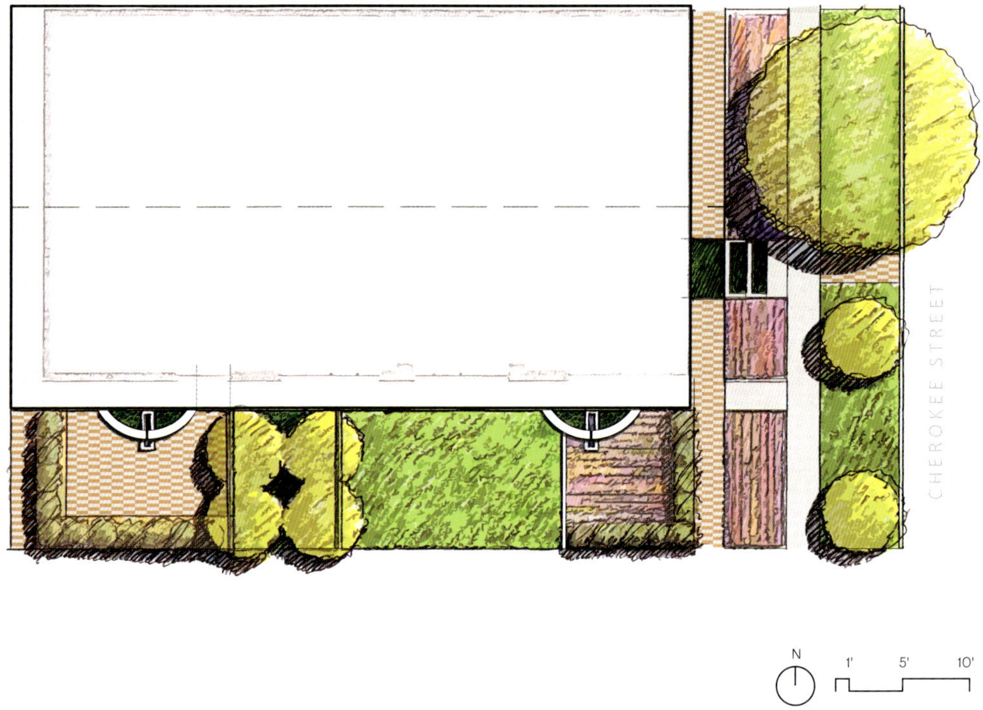


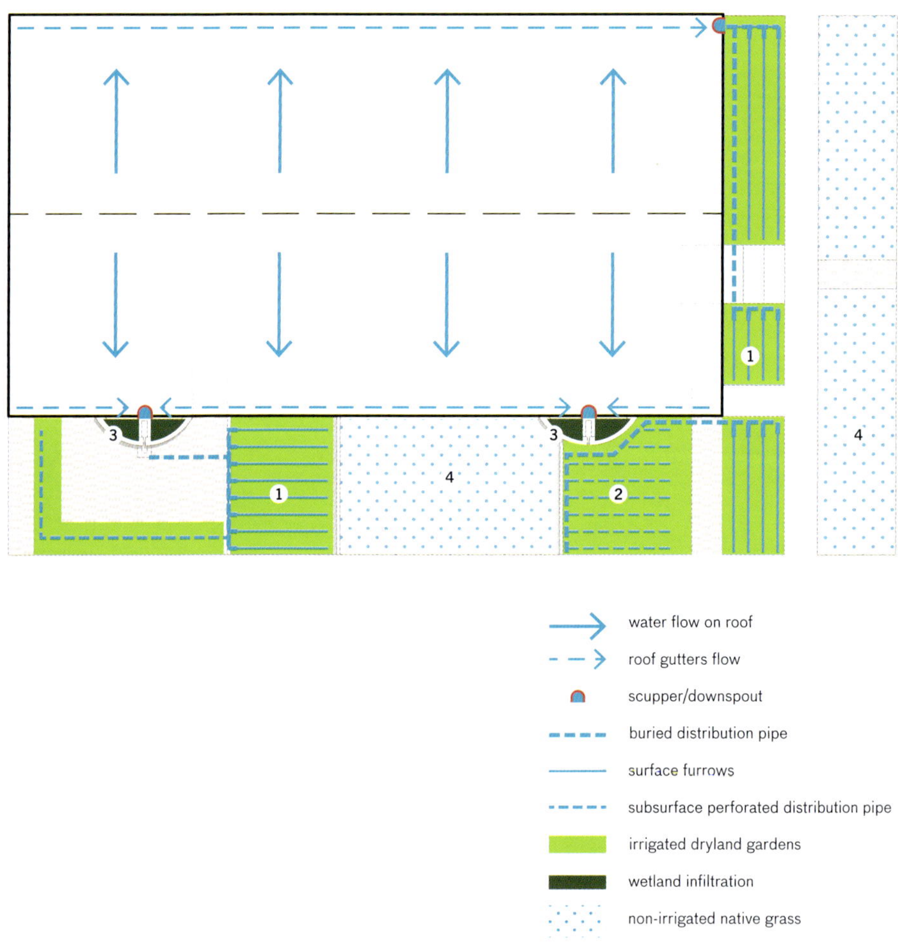


**Garden Site Plan and Water Diagram**

1. A manifold of PVC pipes and furrows mimic the patterns of flood irrigation in agricultural fields distribute rainfall from the roof.
2. The viewing garden is sub-irrigated using perforated PVC pipe running between rows of groundcover plantings.
3. Splash blocks below each downspout direct rainfall into a drain inlet connecting to the distribution piping systems.
4. Prairie and meadow gardens receive only direct rainfall except for garden overflow in extreme rainfall events and through occasional flood irrigation.

Opposite: Water from an overhead downspout is distributed through subsurface and surface systems.

# Northside Park

Denver, Colorado

**Northside Park demonstrates how the most unlikely infrastructure can be repurposed to add community value. The project integrates conventional park design, natural area establishment, and water quality treatment.**

The intrinsic beauty of the finely crafted concrete infrastructure and the monumental scale of the abandoned sewage treatment plant became the primary framework for a new park on the edge of the South Platte River in North Denver.

Built in the 1930s and then decommissioned in the early 1980s, the thirteen-acre Northside Wastewater Treatment Plant sat unused for decades. The stigma of the plant's original use—to treat human waste—and the high cost of demolition discouraged redevelopment. Eventually the site became blighted, vandalized, and covered in graffiti. The idea for adaptive reuse of the site as a park grew out of an environmental settlement in 1987, after residents sued a mining company for contaminating the soil in surrounding neighborhoods and industrial areas with airborne lead from a smelter. The mining company settlement was applied to federal and state funds set aside to clean up a nearby Superfund site and to construct Northside Park as compensation for the long-term impacts on nearby neighborhoods due to industrial operations.

The City and County of Denver's initial concepts proposed completely razing the site and developing a more traditional park and playing fields, but this was determined to be cost-prohibitive. Concepts to repurpose the existing structures for other uses were also rejected due to cost and the lack of a suitable alternative use. To make the construction of a park on the site financially feasible, Wenk Associates used a "design by subtraction" approach that retained and repurposed select components of the plant infrastructure for park use. This strategy reduced construction costs by 30 percent compared to estimates for the treatment plant's complete demolition. To further reduce costs, salvaged steel reinforcement and other structural elements not used for park elements were recycled at a plant within view of the park.

As part of the design process, an adjacent concrete-lined drainage channel was removed and stormwater from adjacent neighborhoods was rerouted through the park. Instead of the concrete channel, a series of wetlands now bring the natural qualities of an adjacent stormwater detention pond into the park and improve the quality of storm runoff flowing into the South Platte River.

Right: The Northside Wastewater Treatment Plant was decommissioned and abandoned in the early 1980s.

Opposite: The structural concrete skeleton creates a functional framework for playfields, picnic areas, seating, and shaded groves.

Above: Conceptual drawing of the final design concept.

Left: The park approximately five years after construction.

**Northside Park Existing Conditions, Site Plan, and Water Diagram**
Opposite, lower left: A concrete-lined storm drain channel directs water around the original treatment plant site. Photo credit: Google Earth, June 1993

Opposite, top: The illustrative plan shows the plant repurposed for park uses.

Opposite, lower right: The rerouted stormwater channel and wetlands now form the western edge of the park, improving the quality of runoff from adjacent neighborhoods and bringing the natural qualities of the nearby the South Platte River into the park.

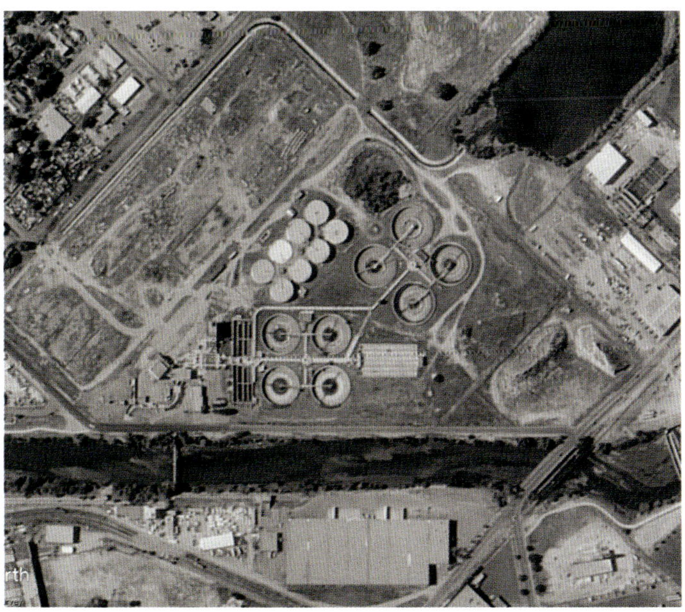

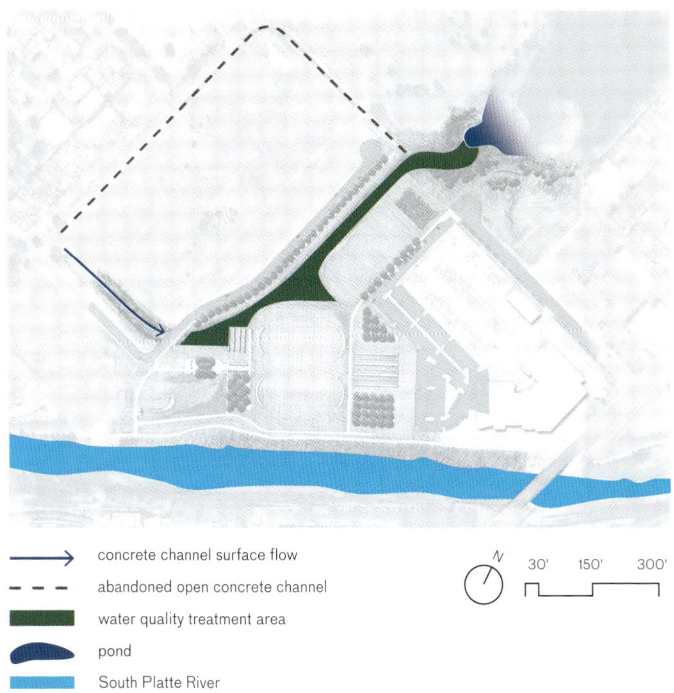
concrete channel surface flow
abandoned open concrete channel
water quality treatment area
pond
South Platte River
N
30'
150'
300'

Above: Mixing basin before construction.

Right: Mature trees now shade informal seating in a grove in a filled mixing basin. Rubble generated during demolition of the plant was used to fill mixing basins to create park spaces and exposed basin walls define plaza areas.

Above: Conceptual sketch and realization of repurposed structures.

Opposite: Because of its isolated location and access barriers, the park receives limited use. Graffiti throughout underscores the need for more intensive park programming and the addition of destination uses that would bring daily activity to the park. To address these issues, the park's natural areas are being expanded, and a center for environmental education will be located on the site to support the park's long-term success.

Northside Park

# Confluence Park

Denver, Colorado

**The renovation of Shoemaker Plaza allows everyone to come safely to the river's edge. Future phases will demonstrate the integration of urban uses and natural technologies to improve water quality and enhance the river's habitat value.**

Opposite, lower left: The confluence of Cherry Creek and the South Platte River around 1970, before construction of Confluence Park and Shoemaker Plaza. Photo credit: Courtesy of Denver Public Library

Opposite, lower right: Shoemaker Plaza, around 1990. Before reconstruction, Narrow ramps, vertical walls and multiple terraces limited use. The regional trail and water access were difficult and unsafe. Right photo credit: ECI Construction

Opposite, top: South Platte RiverFest, June 2018.

Next spread: Shoemaker Plaza today. Photo credit: Brad Nicol Photography

Situated at the confluence of Cherry Creek and the South Platte River, Confluence Park marks the birthplace of Denver, a place where people have gathered for centuries. It was the first major park to be built on the riverfront in the early 1970s, and along with a new regional riverside trail, it was the centerpiece of the revitalization of the South Platte River. Confluence Park was one of the earliest "greenway" projects in the country.

By 2010, new urban neighborhoods, destination retail, regional entertainment and sports venues, and thousands of residents living nearby had transformed the area from aging industrial and rail uses to one of the liveliest and most vital districts in Denver. Dramatic increases in the levels and types of recreation along the river and a need for better access to the regional trail, along with the city's desire to create a greater diversity of activities along the river, required a comprehensive assessment of the park's design and a master plan for its revitalization.

Park revitalization began in 2012 with the preparation of a master plan and the reconstruction of Shoemaker Plaza, the most visible and iconic portion of Confluence Park. The existing plaza required significant upgrades to improve accessibility and needed to be redesigned to allow greater flexibility for a broader range of scheduled events and day-to-day activities.

The reconstruction of Shoemaker Plaza was completed in 2018. Today, an easy-to-navigate pedestrian ramp welcomes visitors to the river's edge and improves bicycle and pedestrian access to the South Platte River Trail. Vertical walls that made river access difficult were replaced by seating terraces stepping down from street level into the river. The new plaza provides safe access to the water's edge, multiple opportunities for informal gathering and relaxation, and a lawn area set within the seating terraces to accommodate larger events.

Future phases of the master plan propose reconstruction of the existing whitewater boating course to improve river access for water sports as part of the removal of an existing dam, and rerouting minor river flows through water quality treatment areas in the Shoemaker Plaza expansion. These improvements will further the city's long-term vision of making the South Platte River clean enough to be fishable and swimmable for all.

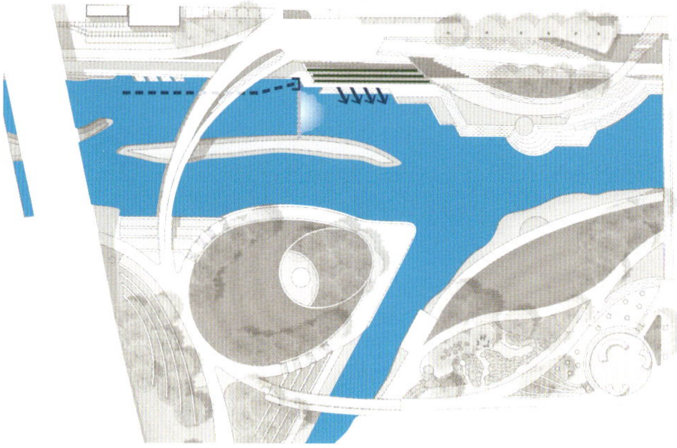

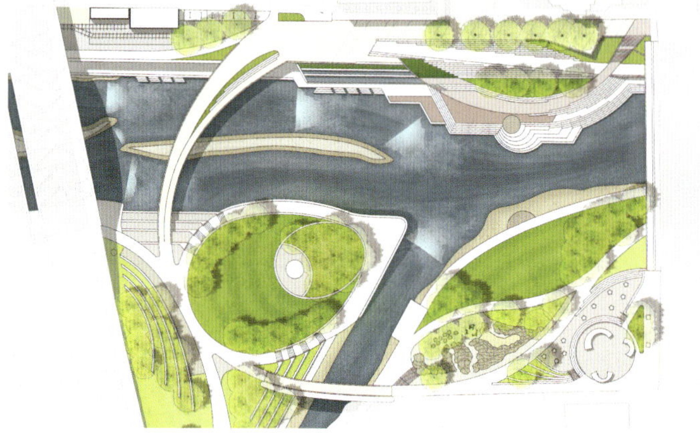

subsurface collection pipe

channel diversion structure

low dam

water quality treatment terraces

discharge of clean water

South Platte River and Cherry Creek

N

10' 50' 100'

**Confluence Park Master Site Plan and Water Diagram**
In a future phase, water quality treatment terraces allow safe waterplay for all.

Right: Master plan illustration of planted water quality terraces proposed as part of a future phase. The rerouting of minor river flows through planted terraces demonstrate how natural technologies can be used to clean river water and allow safe access.

Opposite, top: Long-term proposals for Confluence Park include replacing existing bridge structures to accommodate higher levels of use, as destinations for river viewing and special events. Rendering Credit: AMD Architects

RIVERS FLOW

# Shop Creek

Cherry Creek State Park,
Aurora, Colorado

**The rehabilitation of Shop Creek demonstrates how natural forms, materials, and processes can inspire the redesign of standardized engineering structures to integrate stream channel reconstruction into a visually and naturally sensitive prairie landscape. Constructed in 1989, the project is one of the earliest water quality projects in the region.**

The Shop Creek watershed lies within the gently undulating native prairie near Cherry Creek Reservoir, which is located within a large state park at the edge of Denver. As the city grew around the reservoir, upstream development led to the expansion of impervious surfaces within the watershed, which greatly increased the volume and frequency of stormwater runoff. This in turn precipitated significant algae blooms, fish die-off, and problems for swimmers, boaters, and anglers. The creek's environmental and visual sensitivity required close collaboration between project engineers and landscape architects to develop new approaches to stream channel design to transform the deeply eroded stream into a stable and ecologically diverse waterway that was carefully integrated into the prairie landscape.

Before upstream development occurred, Shop Creek rarely, if ever, conveyed water. Most if not all of the rainfall runoff in the watershed infiltrated into sandy soils before it reached the creek channel. The design team determined that when it came to stabilizing the steeply sloping channel, their options were limited to the construction of grade-control structures—a series of small dams that stairstep down the slope to slow the increased volume and velocity of storm runoff. Given the site's sensitive setting, use of typical standardized grade control structures for channel stabilization were not acceptable. Traditional channel design also limited the ability to take advantage of the increased stream flows to establish wetland habitat and to reduce the flow of phosphorus-rich soil and contaminated urban runoff that contributed to phosphorus pollution in the reservoir.

The solution to restoring Shop Creek was a radical departure from standard channel design. New forms and materials identified for the design of the grade control structures were inspired by prairie and desert streams found in natural sandstone formations. The natural crescent forms that we developed mimic natural stream courses and are highly efficient in reducing the velocity and erosion that results with increased runoff during storm events. The stream channel connecting the structures forms as a series of low terraces designed to establish diverse riparian and wetland plant communities, and landforms typical of the surrounding prairie guide the design of channel edges.

Rather than using the poured-in-place concrete of standard grade control structures, sandy soil found along the creek channel combines with Portland cement to make up the crescent-shaped grade control structures. The resulting soil cement further integrates the structures into the natural surroundings, so that they visually "nest" into the prairie landscape and mimic natural erosion processes.

Constructed in 1989, the Shop Creek restoration project is one of the earliest water quality improvement projects implemented in the region. Monitoring of the project over time confirms the project has met a project goal of removing 80 percent of the creek's total suspended solids (50 percent of which was phosphorus). The project demonstrates how regional forms and materials can inspire new approaches to the design of urban infrastructure to be more context sensitive and safer in a way that encourages park visitors to explore and enjoy nature and natural processes in the city.

Opposite: Six crescent-shaped erosion control structures stabilize the channel.

Above: The structures mimic natural desert stream forms and replace standardized structures.

Left: The eroded Shop Creek channel before stabilization (circa 1987).

Above: Sketch plan rendering of drop structures and plantings

1. low flow channel
2. plunge pool
3. soil cement drop structure
4. dryland grasses
5. wetland grasses
6. cattails and sedges
7. shrub willow

Right: Naturally occurring erosion found in sandstone formations along desert and high plains streams inspired the channel structures and landforms at Shop Creek.

Opposite, top: Soil cement, a mixture of site soil and Portland cement, forms the crescent-shaped structures.

Opposite, bottom: Shop Creek during construction.

**Drop Structure Construction**
Typical plan and section.

**Stream Channel Section**
A series of terraces linking each of the drop structures were planted with riparian and wetland plantings, providing habitat, and promoting the bio-uptake of contaminants that once flowed to the reservoir.

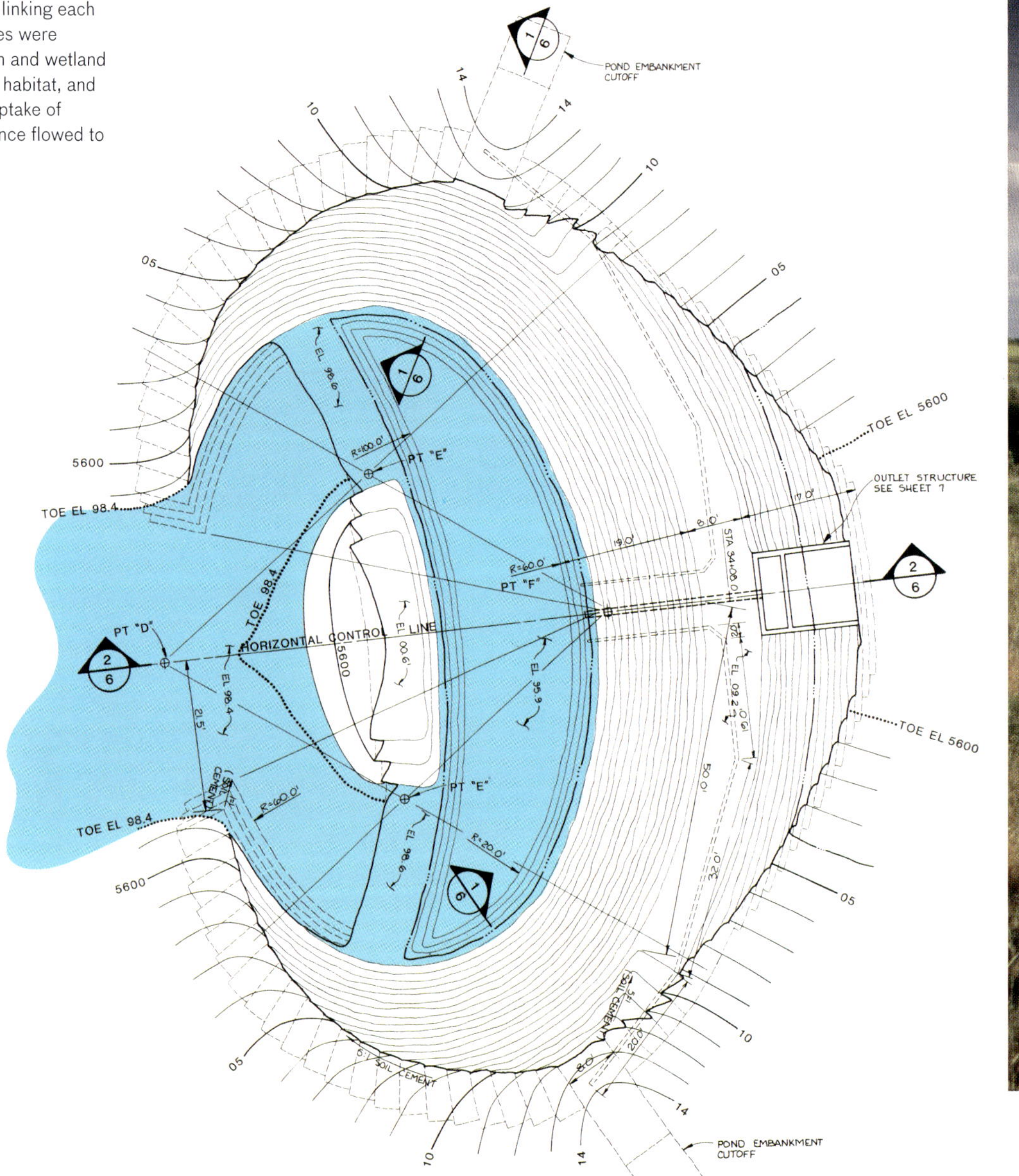


DETAIL B
POND EMBANKMENT PLAN

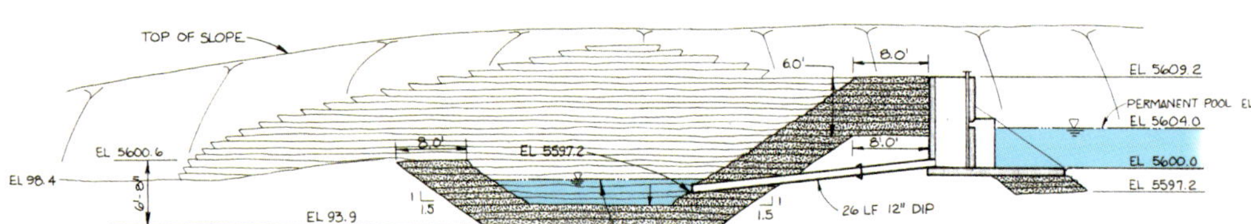


POND EMBANKMENT ℄ 2/6
Scale: 1"=10'

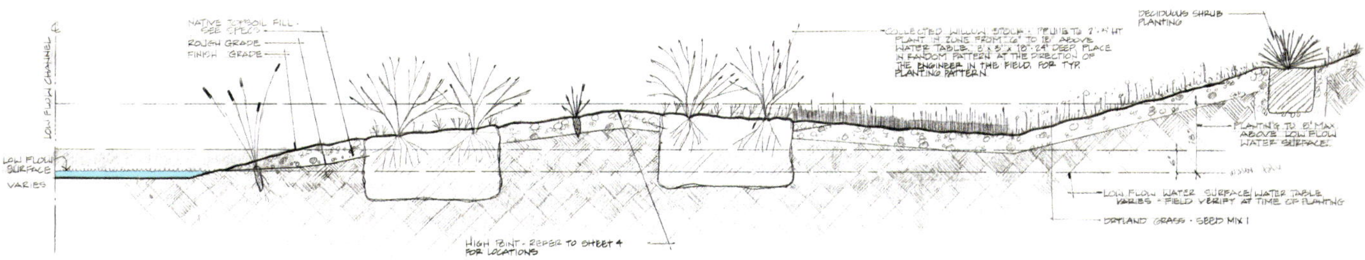


TYPICAL PLANTING SECTION TYPE B CHANNEL BOTTOM

NOT TO SCALE

Above: View of Shop Creek looking upstream following construction (1989).

Below: Willows and cattails established on the channel's bottom terraces three to five years after construction.

Right: Shop Creek today.

# Burgess Creek Promenade

Steamboat Ski Resort,
Steamboat Springs, Colorado

**Partial daylighting of Burgess Creek at the Steamboat Resort base area demonstrates the integration of gray and green infrastructure by diverting portions of the creek to create a community amenity, while maintaining an existing culvert to contain seasonal flows.**

In its natural state, Burgess Creek is a mountain stream that tumbles down the steep slopes of Mount Werner near Steamboat Springs in western Colorado. In the early 1970s, the Steamboat Springs ski resort was constructed, requiring massive grading to build the ski runs and the base area village and the burying of Burgess Creek in a pipe beneath the slopes. The beauty and allure of the mountain stream was lost.

Prior to recent redevelopment, the base area village lacked a strong sense of place. Few visitors chose to spend time there because poor pedestrian connections made access to shops and restaurants difficult and uninviting. The base area was a landscape dominated by roads, parking, and ski slopes with little summertime use.

To make the base area a more desirable destination for visitors and town residents, and to improve its pedestrian connections and walkability, a comprehensive plan was prepared. The plan creates a primary destination for gathering and leisure through the development of a pedestrian promenade at the base of the ski slope. The promenade links shops, restaurants, and hotels in the village and brings the natural qualities of the surrounding mountains into the village by diverting a small portion of Burgess Creek through a surface channel at its edge.

The promenade has become a central gathering place at the heart of the village. A small stream now flows freely in the summertime along the edge of the ski slopes. It cascades through pools and riffles designed to mimic the original stream and natural geology of the surrounding mountain landscape. Each fall, the daylighted stream diverts back into the culvert buried beneath the ski slopes. Snow covers the surface channel in the winter to allow for skiing over the buried stream throughout the ski season.

The addition of the promenade and the lure of the water brought renewed life and economic vitality to the mountain village. The base area is an immensely popular summer destination for visitors and town residents, and is a frequent setting for weddings, large and small concerts, and informal gatherings in all seasons.

**Burgess Creek Plan and Water Diagrams (Summer and Winter)**
In the summer, Burgess Creek runs through pools and riffles alongside a pedestrian promenade. In the winter, surface flows are diverted back into the original buried culvert and the channel is buried in snow to allow for skiing over the stream.

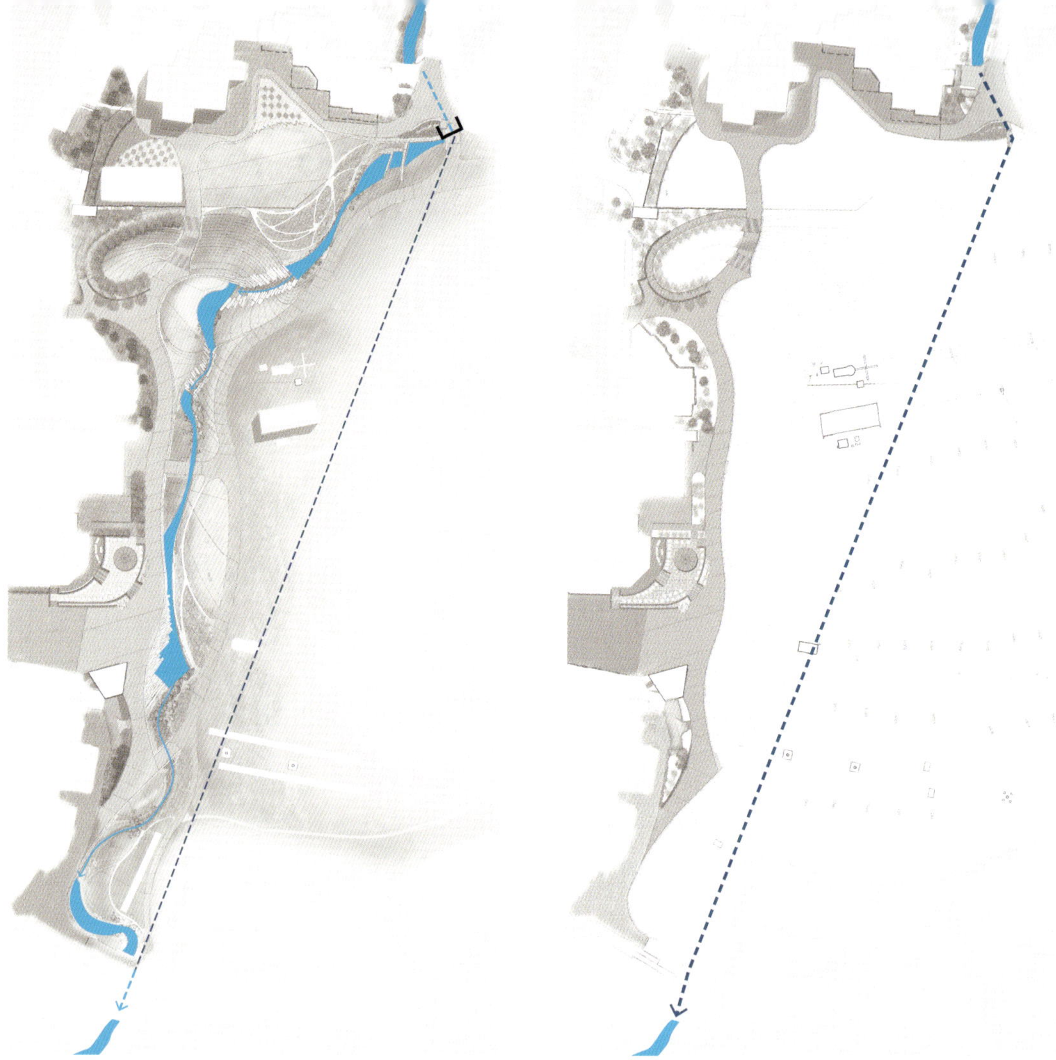

Opposite, lower left: Before redevelopment, the base area lacked a sense of place and pedestrian connections within the village were limited.

Top: Sketch of proposed improvements.

Opposite, top and lower right: Burgess Creek Promenade today in the summer and winter.

Right: Materials mimic the geology of the surrounding mountains.

# The Blue Riverwalk

Breckenridge, Colorado

**Restoring the natural functions of a mined-out riverbed in the heart of a resort community in the Colorado mountains was the key to creating a vibrant public gathering place for the town.**

In the late nineteenth and early twentieth centuries, dredge mining operations to extract gold, silver, and other precious metals devastated the Blue River Valley in and around the mining town of Breckenridge, Colorado. Following decades of neglect after mining operations ceased, the town gradually evolved to become a premier mountain resort with a large year-round permanent resident population. In the 1990s, the Town of Breckenridge recognized the river's potential as a recreational and civic amenity, and undertook a series of projects to improve its cultural, civic, and natural environment. The project included the construction of a new performing arts center, a town square and central green, and a riverwalk along a restored portion of the Blue River to create a community gathering place in the heart of the downtown.

The first step was to restore the river—rehabilitating its ecological function and bringing back its natural qualities. During the hydraulic mining process, miners dredged the river valley, leaving mounds of cobble, a narrow river channel, and soils so poor and rocky that the valley could no longer restore itself. Wenk Associates collaborated with the design team, including engineers and ecologists, to restore the channel's ecological function. To create a soil profile capable of supporting a diverse natural edge and to maintain a constant water level and year-round flow, a polyethylene liner was placed four to five feet below the new channel bottom. Local boulders, cobble, and gravel were used to create a natural riffle/pool sequence. Topsoil salvaged from construction sites in the valley, and locally sourced plant materials were used to restore the native riparian and alpine plant communities typical of the area, an important factor given the town's extreme climate at an elevation of 9,600 feet.

The new downtown riverfront along the restored river became the town's center for community gathering and celebration, and a regional destination for festivals, concerts, conferences, and special community events. Native trout naturally repopulated the river, and native plant communities now thrive along its banks. The success of the project encouraged the revitalization and redevelopment of underused properties along the river. Over two decades later, the Blue Riverwalk remains the iconic center for year-round activity in Breckenridge's historic downtown.

Right: Dredge mining operations devastated the Blue River Valley. Vast areas of dredge rock, visible on the left edge of the photo, remain downriver of the town today. Photo credit: Denver Public Library, Western History Collection, X-1973

Opposite: After restoration.

Opposite, top series: The river channel 1) prior to construction, 2) during the installation of the polyethylene liner and topsoil, and 3) following construction.

Opposite, bottom: The restored Blue River at the Riverwalk Center performing arts venue (2017).

Above: The Riverwalk links Main Street businesses to parking and residential areas and integrates utility corridors, emergency, and service access.

Left: Industrial and natural materials recall the historic structures typical of the town's mining past.

Next spread: The restored river, central green, and town square.

# River North Park and Promenade

Denver, Colorado

**The repurposing of existing buildings and infrastructure along the South Platte River is the framework for a new neighborhood park that will be a destination for the creative and performing arts. The integration of green infrastructure into traditional park spaces supports plantings that reflect the natural qualities of the adjacent South Platte River.**

Opposite, top: Stormwater treatment meadows support the plantings that are native to the nearby river.

Opposite, bottom: The River North Park and Promenade prior to construction and conceptual completion.

The River North (RiNo) district in central Denver, once a run-down industrial backwater and a favored location for artists for decades, has become one of the most diverse and eclectic mixed-use neighborhoods in the city. Over the past several years, thousands of new residential units, and dozens of new restaurants, shops, and offices have been developed in the area, and it continues to be an important center for the creative arts. Because of the area's history of industrial use, no parks were ever built there. The South Platte River, the only natural feature and public open space in the area, passes through the heart of the district, but access to the river and to the regional trail along its banks is severely limited, blocked by roads, rail lines, and large industrial uses. As development in the RiNo began to increase, the community spoke out for their desire for a park that would reflect and retain the gritty character and historic structures of the neighborhood.

The city responded by repurposing an existing city maintenance shop site and its buildings as a new urban park along the South Platte River, and transforming an adjacent seldom-used street paralleling the river into a pedestrian promenade. Combined, the River North Park and Promenade will bring a much-needed urban gathering place to the neighborhood that will support the creative culture of the district and be an extension of the emerging entertainment and restaurant scene.

In response to the community's wishes, the existing buildings on the park site will be converted into flexible spaces for community gatherings, cultural events, and a collaborative art studio and maker's space that will be managed by the RiNo Arts District. The RiNo Arts District's commitment to the creative programming of the reused buildings will result in a center for the neighborhood's creative endeavors, leisure activities, and recreation. More traditional park elements and a variety of performance spaces are set within groves of cottonwoods and riparian meadows supported by stormwater runoff from the neighborhood and integral to the park and promenade, connecting them to the natural qualities of the adjacent river.

For RiNo Promenade, which extends along nine blocks of riverfront, remnants of the existing roadway will remain, and asphalt will be selectively removed to provide space for plantings, seating, and gathering. The design of the promenade has been coordinated with existing and proposed uses of adjacent private development to blur the edges between public and private space, and to create a lively and interesting corridor to walk, sit, eat, and be entertained, all in the heart of Denver's funkiest neighborhood overlooking the South Platte River Greenway.

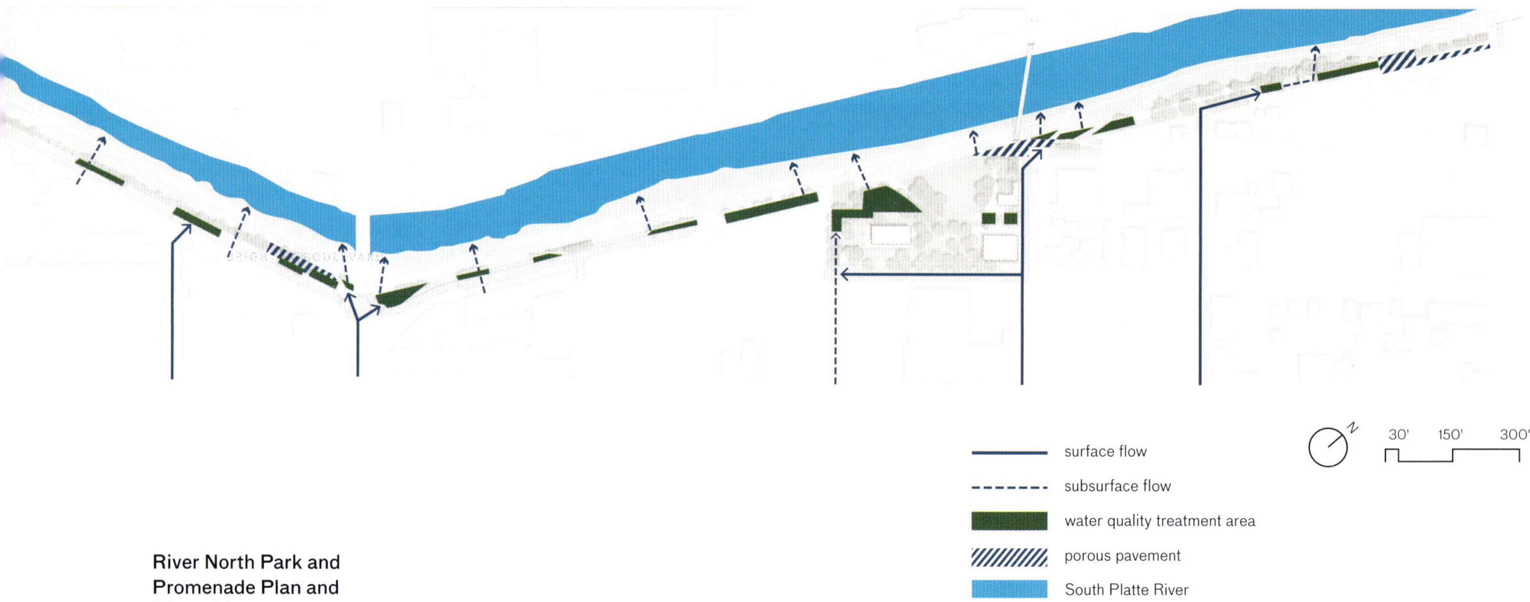


**River North Park and Promenade Plan and Water Diagram**
Stormwater is conveyed from nearby streets to a series of biofilters in the park and promenade.

Opposite, top: Existing maintenance shops will be repurposed and selectively demolished to integrate building and park uses.

Opposite, bottom: An elevated walkway overlooks the river and the promenade.

Next spread: The River Promenade will repurpose an existing street and become an integral part of adjacent private development.

# TAXI Mixed-Use Development

Denver, Colorado

**TAXI is a mixed-use urban village situated in a naturalized landscape and integrated with surface stormwater controls that bring the character of the adjacent South Platte River into the site. Parking areas and drives integrate into the site's landscape and gathering areas to enhance its sense of community.**

The River North (RiNo) district in Denver was an aging industrial neighborhood of warehouses, manufacturing facilities, trucking terminals, and rail switch yards located along the South Platte River. In recent years, the district has undergone dramatic changes as artists and makers convert derelict buildings into a thriving arts district. TAXI was one of the first mixed-use developments in RiNo, and is home to a creative community of artists, start-up businesses, and designers in a live/work environment. Its design recalls the area's industrial history and former operations as a taxi dispatch center, and the landscape celebrates the qualities of the natural river landscape.

Almost twenty years ago, the client, an adventurous developer known for his pioneering developments in aging and underused urban neighborhoods, saw the potential of RiNo, an area where artists and other creative enterprises were already beginning to locate. To attract creative businesses and artists to TAXI, he knew the rents must be affordable and the development should integrate the qualities of the natural environment, employ sustainable practices, celebrate the area's gritty industrial past, and provide connections to the adjacent South Platte River.

The project was well underway when the developer engaged Wenk Associates to rethink the site's challenging stormwater infrastructure issues. The essentially flat existing terrain made drainage difficult and potentially costly, and the surface parking that would cover much of the site was a requirement to keep the project affordable. To minimize costs and to take full advantage of the site's infrastructure, multiple-benefit solutions to the challenges were identified through a site plan that integrates parking, pedestrian spaces, and landscape areas into a surface stormwater system. The green infrastructure approach to stormwater management provided multiple benefits: 1) it eliminated the need to import fill material (which would have been required to create positive drainage for a traditional piped system) as well as almost all subsurface storm pipe, contributing to significant cost reductions; and 2) the stormwater that would be captured and infiltrated would support the desired landscape, which brings the natural qualities of the nearby river into the site.

Today, TAXI is a twenty-five-acre urban village, a home and workplace for artists, architects, designers, and "creative class" business startups, with a café, daycare, and gathering areas integrated into groves and meadows sustained by the site's stormwater system. TAXI has been the catalyst for the rapid transformation of the area into one of the hippest urban neighborhoods in Denver.

Opposite: The site uses an interconnected system of green infrastructure as its primary means of managing on-site stormwater.
Photo credit: Alan Brown, Zeppelin Development

Left: Prior to redevelopment, the site was a former landfill and taxi storage and dispatch center.

Above: The use of low-cost native plants, seeded native grasses, painted pedestrian walkways integrated into access drives, and the use of green infrastructure as the primary means of stormwater management supports a walkable environment. This approach significantly reduced site development costs.

**TAXI Site Plan and Water Diagram at Full Build-Out**
Covered surface channels, grass swales, and stormwater infiltration gardens convey and treat runoff from adjacent buildings and parking areas, eliminating the need for costly subsurface storm pipes and curb and gutter.

Opposite: Plantings of cottonwoods, native grasses, and wildflowers connect the site to the nearby river, and are accessible to first-floor tenants.

Site furnishings are fashioned from industrial materials manufactured nearby or from recycled sources.

# Lowry Parks and Open Space

Former Lowry Air Force Base, Denver, Colorado

**The redevelopment of a former Air Force base demonstrates how restoring a buried creek and repurposing stormwater infrastructure to make the site more multifunctional can create important open-space assets for a new community development.**

Opposite, top: Stormwater outfall. A large box culvert discharges major storm flows through the metal grates in this small grade control structure.

Opposite, bottom: Lowry Air Force Base circa 1945. The mixed-use community that replaced the Base lies between historic neighborhoods and post –World War II suburbs in the heart of the Denver metropolitan area. Photo Credit: USGOV-PD

For fifty-seven years, Lowry Air Force Base served the country first as an airfield preparing soldiers for combat through multiple wars, and later as a technical training center for the U.S. military. When the base was decommissioned in 1994, ownership was transferred to the City of Denver for redevelopment as a new mixed-use urbanist community located on the eastern edge of the city. Vast piles of rubble from runway demolition, contaminated soils and groundwater, and a buried creek presented special challenges and opportunities for development of the community's 230-acre park and open-space system. Westerly Creek had been buried for decades beneath extensive runways, as required for base operations. As Denver grew around it, flooding increased on Westerly Creek, leading to the construction of two regional stormwater detention basins on the base.

Two primary goals of the redevelopment project were to daylight and restore the natural qualities of Westerly Creek as the park system's spine, and to integrate the existing detention basins as open-space amenities. The daylighted creek was designed to function as part of the city's stormwater system for regional and local flood conveyance, as well as the community's local stormwater conveyance and treatment system. Local stormwater runoff is treated in extensive riparian and wetland areas, which are an integral part of park designs.

Another goal of the park plan was to integrate Denver's early-twentieth-century "City Beautiful" park design traditions with more regionally appropriate, water-conservative park types that recognize the natural and recreational values of open space. Traditional recreation and park facilities, which included athletic fields, play areas, picnicking, and community gathering spaces are limited to more intensively maintained areas. Lower maintenance, lower water-use natural areas, that mimic the natural qualities of the High Plains, integrate stormwater treatment areas and create a rich mosaic of wetland, riparian, and upland areas linked by an extensive trail network that complements the active-use park areas.

There are three primary areas in the Lowry parks and open-space system:

**The Fillets at the Westerly Creek Dam.** The Westerly Creek Dam, a forty-foot-high, three-mile-long flood control structure, was constructed decades ago to reduce flooding in established neighborhoods downstream. The top of the dam can now be accessed by way of "fillets," a term we coined to describe sculptural pedestrian ramps, constructed using thousands of cubic yards of concrete rubble left over from airfield demolition. The dam provides expansive views of the mountains and city, as well as regional trail connections for Lowry and the surrounding communities. Miles of existing maintenance roads around the detention basin and across the dam had the potential to become a valuable extension of the park system's trail network if adequate connections could be established. The rubble proved to be a convenient resource to construct the two monumental fillets at strategic points along the dam to connect the detention area maintenance roads to the park system's trails. The system's spine and natural areas are now an integral part of the community's extensive park, trails, and open-space network.

**The Lowry Sports Complex.** The Lowry Sports Complex is one of Denver's premier sports parks for adult and youth recreational leagues. The complex features multi-use playing fields, soccer fields, and court sports organized along Sports Boulevard, a mile-long spine that minimizes site paving through the integration of pedestrian circulation, auto access, and parking. The boulevard provides direct field access and is an integral part of the trail network.

**The Great Lawn.** The Great Lawn is a community park reminiscent of many of Denver's historic City Beautiful–era parks, framed by prairies and multifunctional natural areas. At the park's center is a large events lawn. Gently undulating prairies, water-quality wetlands, and a network of trails surround the lawn. Roughly half of the park's land area is prairie, or wetlands sustained by stormwater runoff from the Lowry Town Center. The daylighted and restored Westerly Creek passes through lawns, ponds, natural areas, and gathering places, each with a distinct character and purpose.

**Lowry Site Plan**

1. Regional stormwater detention
2. Westerly Creek Dam
3. Eastern Fillet
4. Western Fillet
5. Westerly Creek
6. Sports Park
7. Sports Boulevard
8. Great Lawn Park
9. Sundial

**Lowry Water Diagram**

The daylighting of Westerly Creek created a framework for the park system that integrates stormwater treatment, local and regional stormwater detention, and parks.

Far left: View from the dam. Large piles of concrete rubble left from airfield demolition were used for the construction of the Fillets.

Left: Concept sketch of the East Fillet.

Far lower left: Study model of the East Fillet.

Below: View of the east fillet, dam, detention area, and sports complex.
Photo credit: Brad Nicol Photography.

East Fillet and primary access trail.

Top and bottom: Conceptual sketch of the dam and as constructed with the sports complex in the middle distance.

Opposite, top: Lowry Sports Complex. The East Fillet is visible in the background of the sports fields.

Opposite, bottom: Sports Boulevard integrates local and regional trails and sports field access.

Lowry Parks and Open Space

Top and bottom: The Great Lawn Park sundial serves as a terminus of Denver's historic 6th Avenue Parkway, which links the Lowry parks to Denver's historic park and parkway system. The lawn surrounding it is being used in surprising ways and provides a unique setting for a martial arts class.
Drone photo credit: Brad Nicol Photography.

Opposite: Water quality wetlands, center right, treat runoff from the town center.

Above and right: Gently undulating prairies surround the Great Lawn.

Opposite, top: The Great Lawn overlook is situated at the high point of the park.

Opposite, bottom: Daylighted Westerly Creek.

Next spread: Stormwater outfall in winter.

Lowry Parks and Open Space

# Menomonee Valley Redevelopment

Milwaukee, Wisconsin

**The Menomonee Valley once again provides jobs, parks, and open spaces and a cleaner river for underserved neighborhoods in Milwaukee, restoring its historic role as a working landscape. A system of stormwater controls manages and improves the quality of rainfall flowing from industrial areas, where it is cleaned as it passes through open spaces to the Menomonee River, supporting the restoration of the valley's natural qualities.**

The Menomonee Valley, an aging industrial area near downtown Milwaukee, has a long history as a working landscape. Native Americans harvested wild rice there when it was an expansive marsh at the edge of Lake Michigan. When Europeans settled the area, the marsh was filled, and the river was channelized. By the early twentieth century, the valley had been transformed into one of the most important industrial centers on the Great Lakes and in America, and its natural qualities were lost in the transformation.

Following World War II, industrial uses in the valley declined, and many businesses moved away or went bankrupt. In the 1980s, the Milwaukee Railroad failed, and a 133-acre rail yard and engine maintenance and manufacturing facility remained derelict for two decades. In 2002, Wenk Associates won a national design competition with a concept for the site's revitalization based on restoring the valley as a "working landscape" that mediates between the restoration of the original natural landscape and the revitalization of its industrial past. For the next decade, the City of Milwaukee, the State of Wisconsin, and multiple nonprofit partners worked together to create a sustainably designed industrial center with good jobs, new parks, and ecologically diverse open spaces along the restored Menomonee River. The project would become the largest brownfield redevelopment success in Wisconsin's history.

The goals for the revitalization project were to plan for one million square feet of job-rich, living-wage, light industrial development, and sixty acres of open space and parks that would be connected to adjacent park-deficient neighborhoods. The plan called for a healthier and more resilient pattern of development that would reduce flood risk and clean and infiltrate stormwater runoff from all industrial uses within the redevelopment area. The parks incorporate areas for active recreation and environmental education, and provide access for residents of nearby urban neighborhoods, while the rehabilitated river is more accessible and ecologically diverse.

The redevelopment includes two primary park spaces—Menomonee Valley Community Park and Three Bridges Park—which extend and connect the Hank Aaron State Trail to the downtown and adjacent neighborhoods. The forty-five-acre Community Park creates an extensive open-space network around which the industrial area is organized. The multifunctional stormwater treatment and detention areas in the park retain and filter up to the hundred-year storm event, and also support trails, recreation areas, and functioning natural systems that restore wildlife habitat and improve the quality of stormwater leaving the site. The treatment areas connect to the river and support a linked series of seven landscape types indigenous to southern Wisconsin, ranging from mesic prairie to swamp forest. The park also includes soccer fields, court sports, a skate park, and other destination recreation uses under an existing viaduct.

Three Bridges Park, a twenty-four-acre open space formed by a series of hills created by capping contaminated soil and building debris, mimic the landforms and ecology of Wisconsin's glacial landscapes, recalling the local valleys that once linked the nearby uplands to the river. Three pedestrian bridges and a restored underpass that had once connected the rail yards to adjacent neighborhoods now provide access to the park for nearby residents. The Urban Ecology Center, a community-based nonprofit organization

that focuses on environmental education for inner-city youth, is located next to the park. Both parks provide a learning landscape for the center's environmental education programs and community gardens. The center is also involved in the ongoing restoration and stewardship of the parks' natural areas.

The Menomonee Valley redevelopment has created over 1,400 jobs and provided a new street network connecting the area to the city's street grid and trails linking the valley to surrounding neighborhoods and downtown Milwaukee. Today, the system of parks and open space manages flooding, improves water quality, and sustains extensive natural areas, providing a framework for healthy and active lifestyles as well as access to recreation and nature for residents of the adjacent neighborhoods.

A district stormwater system manages, treats, and infiltrates stormwater from seventy acres of infill development.

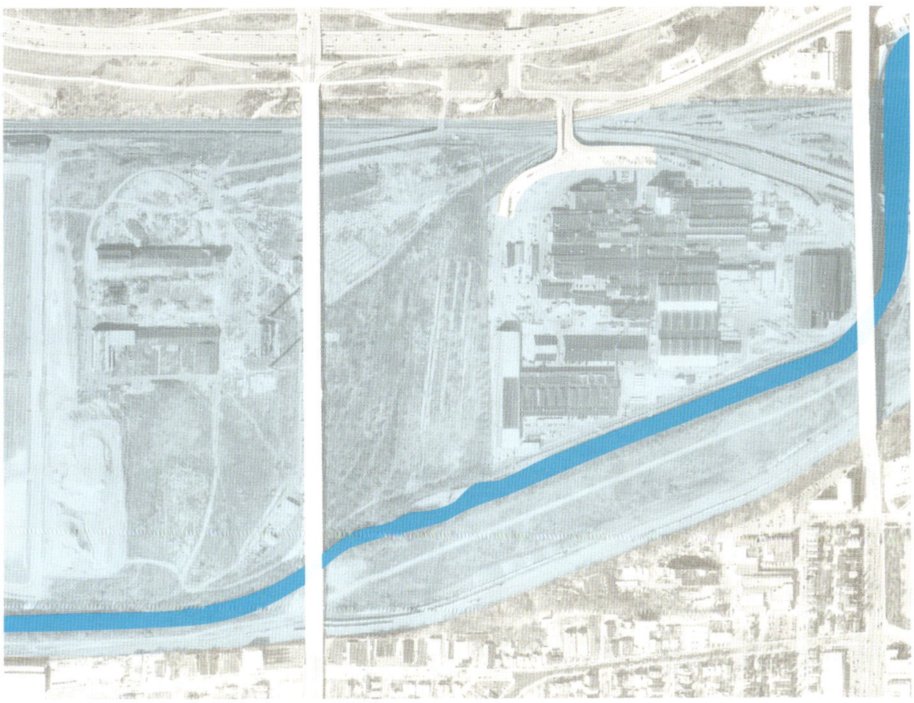

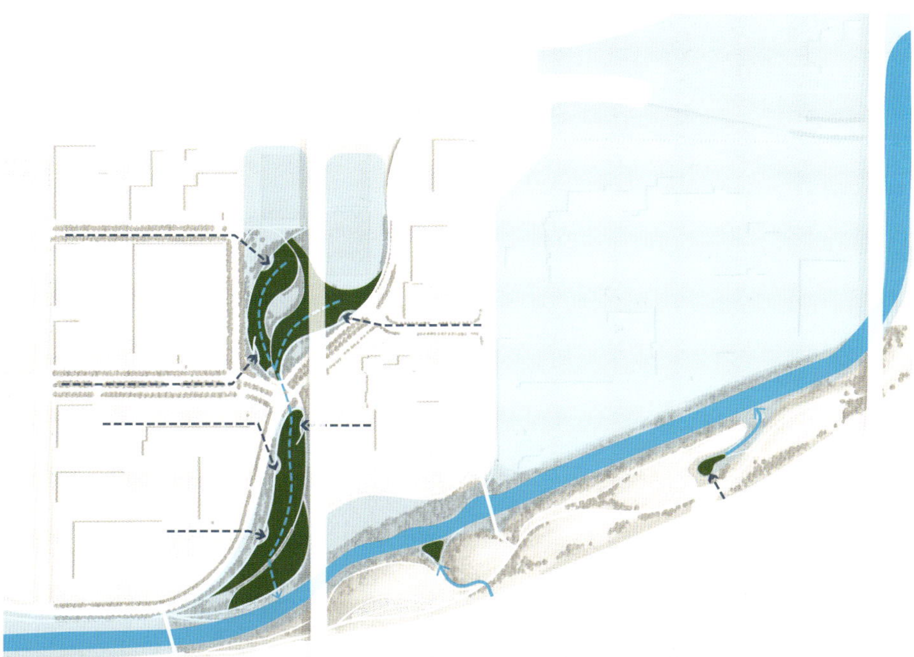

Opposite, top: The 133-acre redevelopment site integrates light industrial development with a new system of parks, open spaces, and regional trail connections. The park system incorporates improved flood control, water quality treatment, and restoration of natural systems.

Opposite, lower left: Extensive marches leading to Lake Michigan once provided food for Native American tribes. Photo credit: Milwaukee County Historical Society.

Opposite, lower right: The Menomonee River Valley circa 1935. Photo credit: Milwaukee County Historical Society.

**Redevelopment Site Plan**

1. Light industrial
2. Menomonee Valley Community Park
3. Three Bridges Park

**Water Diagrams (Before and After Development)**
Consolidation of storm-water treatment in natural areas frees up more land for development and supports the restoration of a functioning floodplain.

subsurface pipe
surface flow
subsurface flow to river
water quality treatment wetlands
Menomonee River
100-year floodplain

N
50' 250' 500'

Above: Regional and local trails have restored historic pedestrian access to the valley.

Right: Soccer fields at Menomonee Valley Community Park. Photo credit: Menomonee Valley Partners

Opposite, top: Destination court sports have yet to be implemented beneath an existing viaduct.

Opposite, bottom: The nonprofit Urban Ecology Center, located adjacent to the parks, is actively involved in the parks' ongoing restoration and stewardship and environmental education.

**Menomonee Valley Community Park Planting Plan**
Stormwater infiltration areas in the park support seven different indigenous Wisconsin landscapes ranging from mesic prairie to swamp forest.

Below: Placement of the layer of concrete rubble during construction and storm runoff following construction. Photo credit: left, City of Milwaukee, and right, Paul Boersma

Opposite: Stormwater treatment areas at Menomonee Valley Community Park. The treatment areas, illustrated in the cross section, which occupy roughly half of the park and retain and infiltrate up to the hundred-year storm event, are constructed over contaminated soils capped with a clay liner, eighteen inches of concrete rubble, and a constructed soil profile that remove eighty percent of total suspended solids from contaminated runoff.

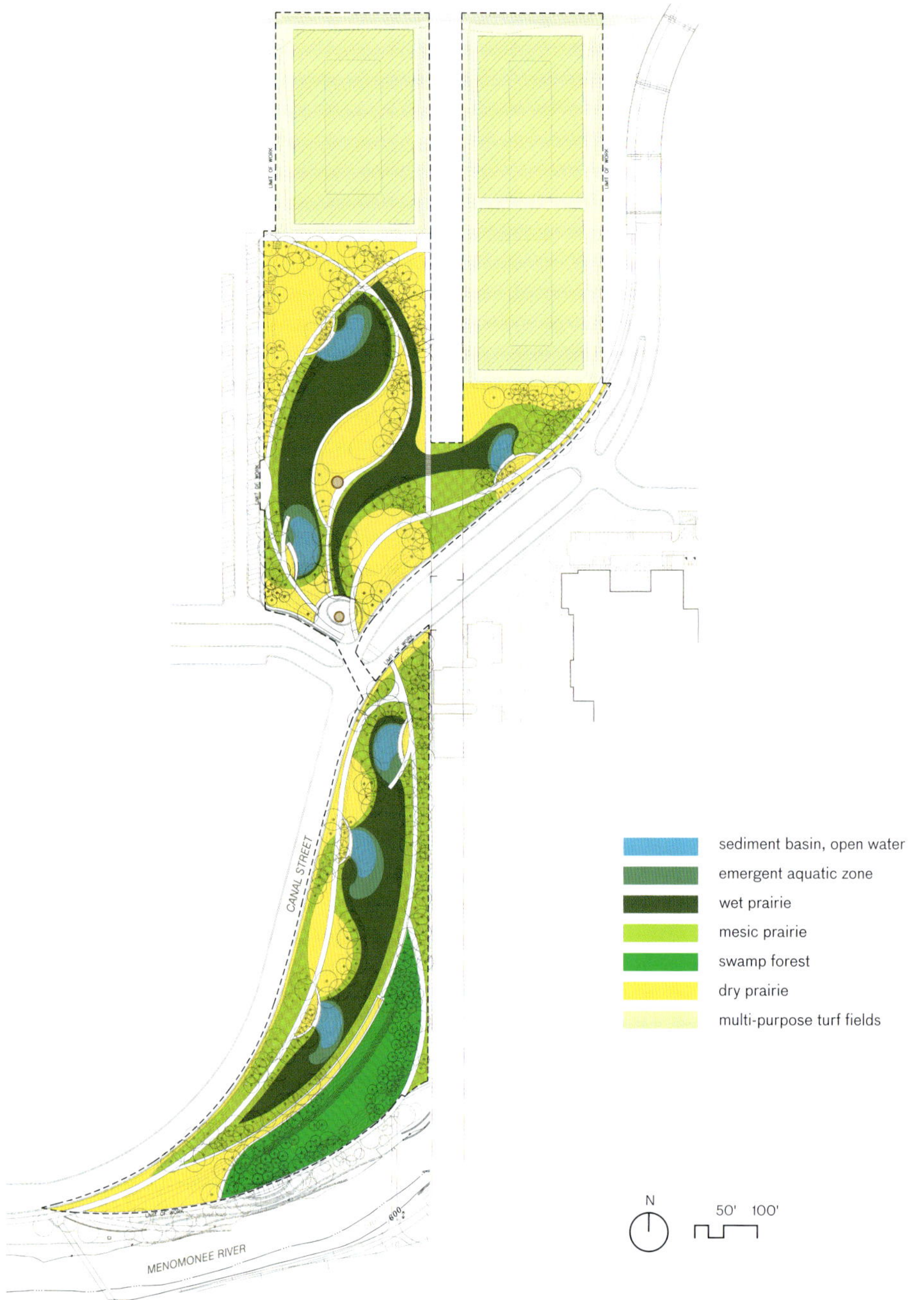

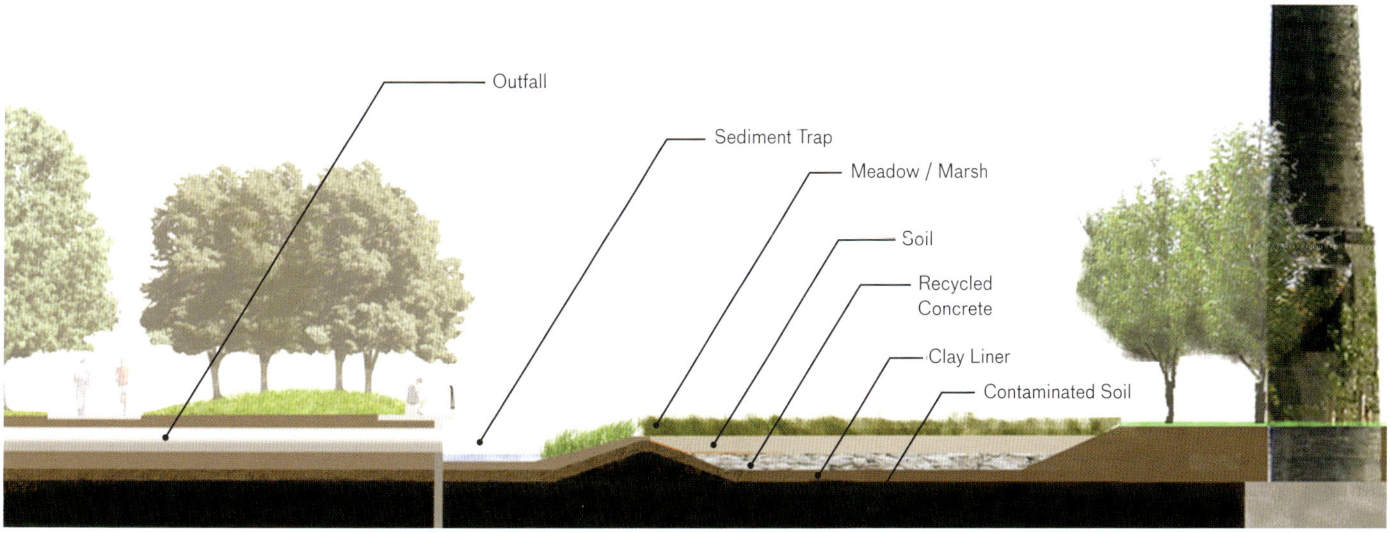
Outfall
Sediment Trap
Meadow / Marsh
Soil
Recycled Concrete
Clay Liner
Contaminated Soil

Aerial views of the Community Park stormwater treatment thirteen years after construction and a four-inch rainstorm. Visible are four different landscape types. Photos credit: Paul Boersma

MASTERSON

Opposite, left: At Three Bridges Park, landforms that mimic the forms and ecology of Wisconsin's glacial landscapes were created by capping vast quantities of contaminated construction rubble and soil prior to shaping and installation of a clay cap and topsoil. Top Photo Credit: MKE Drones. Middle Right Photo Credit: Nairn Okler, Alloy Photography

Opposite, bottom: Urban Ecology Center solar eclipse field trip (August 21, 2017). Photo credit: Adam Carr

Above: Storm runoff from adjacent rail yards sustains an emergent wetland and a calcareous spring pond. Photo Credit: Nairn Okler, Alloy Photography

Left: A prescribed burn. Photo credit: Adam Carr

Next Spread: Three Bridges Park. Photo credit: Adam Carr

# The River Mile

Denver, Colorado

**The River Mile, a proposed sixty-acre urban district along the South Platte River in the heart of Denver, will embrace the river as a place for community gathering and as an important component of a district-wide stormwater management system. Rainfall will become a resource that supports the restoration of the river's natural qualities and that enhances the value of the district's streets and public spaces.**

Through the late nineteenth and early twentieth centuries, Denver grew rapidly, and the project area along the South Platte River in central Denver became an important industrial center and railyard. As a result, the river was channelized and lost its natural qualities. Although the project area was redeveloped in the 1980s to its current use as an amusement park, multiple environmental challenges remain due to the area's industrial past. Currently, the site lies entirely within the hundred-year floodplain because of a buildup of sediment in the river channel caused by a small diversion dam at the downstream edge of the project area.

Future improvements will require the floodplain to be contained within the river channel and will create the opportunity to reconstruct the channel as a functioning natural corridor and community amenity. Lined with urban parks and a pedestrian promenade, the river will define the district's identity as the central gathering place for leisure and civic activities. The urban promenade will connect a series of plazas and parks along the river, weaving the natural fabric of the river into the district and connecting the proposed district to other neighborhoods and parks along the river.

The river's channel construction will mimic its natural sinuosity and restore a continuous riparian and wetland edge. A riffle-pool sequence will support native fish, a sport fishery, and paddle sports. Fingers of the terraced natural river edge will extend into the district, merging urban and natural qualities. The proposed river terraces will be an important part of the district's stormwater system that will reduce the volume and improve the quality of urban runoff and support the establishment of a riparian river edge. These terraces will be part of a comprehensive system of flow reduction techniques, including porous pavements and green roofs, designed to reduce or eliminate the need for large, single-use stormwater detention and treatment facilities throughout the district.

The river terraces will accommodate multiple opportunities for river overlooks, seating, and lawns for recreation. A hierarchy of trails will allow for multiple points of access to the river's edge. The central plaza will host civic celebrations, concerts, and other large programmed events, and be the primary river access point in the district. Because of this access, it will become one of the most important public spaces in the heart of the city.

A system of natural technologies will be an integral part of the River Mile's streets, buildings, parks, and open spaces to manage stormwater and support the restoration of the river corridor's natural functions and qualities.

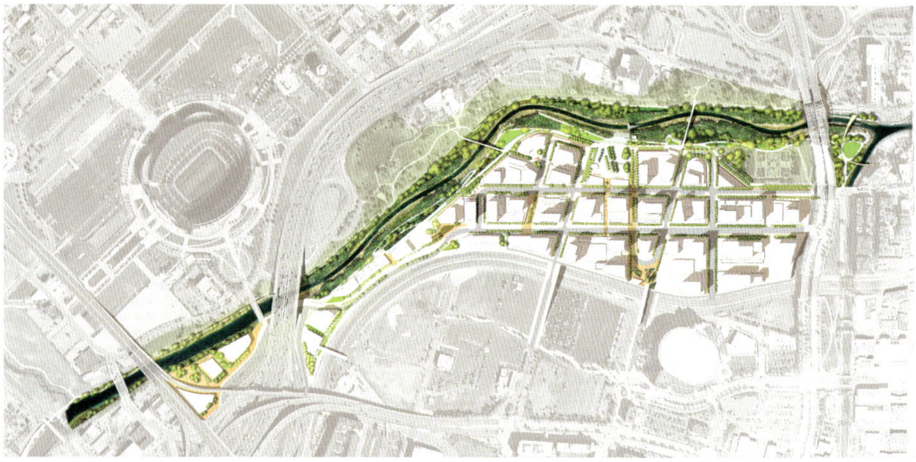

permeable streetscapes

water quality treatment wetlands

rooftop detention and timed release

South Platte River

N

50' 250' 500'

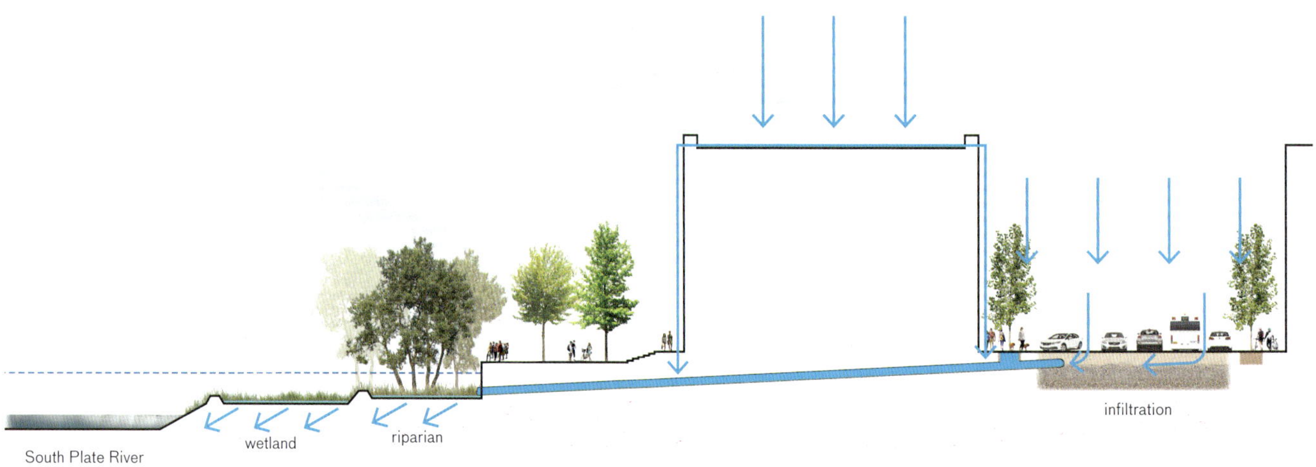

**River Mile Illustrative Plan, Water Plan Diagram, and Water Section**
The need for a traditional piped stormwater system is reduced using natural technologies. Surface stormwater runoff is treated in permeable streets and stormwater planters. Green roofs provide detention, which is piped to sustain wetlands and riparian areas along the river.

Above: River Mile street concept rendering.

Nearly one mile of the South Platte River will be restored as a functioning natural floodplain with multiple environmental and recreational benefits.

# Grand River Corridor

Grand Rapids, Michigan

**The restoration of the Grand River corridor demonstrates how recreation and urban systems, and natural systems and functions of the river edge, can be reestablished and integrated into the heart of the city.**

The city of Grand Rapids has a vision to restore the natural qualities of the Grand River that Charles Belknap, an early nineteenth-century settler of the area, vividly remembered as,

> *where the "wild plum and crabapple trees dotted the island and grapevines wound themselves in the Water Elms… When the Indians set up their wigwams in the spring, they suspended swings for the children on long branches of the great-grandfather of all sycamore trees…"*

Grand Rapids grew quickly in the nineteenth and early twentieth centuries, as numerous industries located along the river's edge, and that intimate relationship between residents and the river was lost. Dams were constructed to generate power for the burgeoning industries, and the river was channelized and walled in. The decline of those industries in the twentieth century prompted the community to rethink the value of the river. In more recent decades, the city has pursued incremental redevelopment of the river's edge with civic, cultural, and private development that is once again bringing the community to the river.

In 2017, the city commissioned a multidisciplinary team to work with their private partners, who were developing plans to restore the river's historic rapids. It was the team's responsibility to reestablish a more direct and intimate relationship between the river, the river's edge, and the community. Goals included balancing expanded recreational use and river access, private redevelopment, and restoration of the river's natural qualities. To guide multiple phases of implementation, design guidelines were developed for trails, parks, and open space for a 7.5-mile segment of the river corridor, and schematic designs were prepared for six new public parks along the riverfront.

To accommodate a large number of boaters and an even greater number of anglers anticipated as part of restoration of the rapids, the guidelines call for partial removal of the existing floodwalls, to establish more direct, universally accessible, and safer connections to the water's edge. The guidelines include protocols for planting concepts to reestablish native plant communities and aquatic, riparian, and upland wildlife habitat. Planting patterns that range from urban to more naturalized establish important habitat connectivity for multiple species, including the most urbanized portions of the city.

Park concepts were developed for each of the six sites along the river to accommodate multiple river-oriented activities, large festivals, playgrounds, court sports, and other activities that would draw people to the river every day. Private development, in partnership with the city, is anticipated to further activate the river by creating important places to live, work, and play to fully realize the Grand River's potential as a "river for all."

A decommissioned water storage site will become a regional riverfront park. An existing storage tank will be repurposed as a special events and performance venue and the park will be one of the primary river access points.

The Grand River corridor project area extends 7.5 miles through the city. It includes downtown Grand Rapids, industrial areas, vacant lots, natural parks, and neighborhoods in transition.

The corridor can be described through four character zones that acknowledge its diversity and history. Design guidelines recognize the uniqueness of each character zone without limiting project goals of establishing a unified corridor identity, improving community connections to the River, and enhancing natural systems along the river.

Schematic designs were developed for the identified Opportunity Sites which were selected as high priority for redevelopment as urban parks to benefit from the expanded recreation potential of the river.

Opposite: Prototypes for Resilient River Edges. In downtown Grand Rapids the river edge is lined almost completely with a floodwall. A range of river edge prototypes were developed to replace the wall and to respond to the opportunities and constraints of different land uses and recreational opportunities along the river's edge.

P1 – Redevelopment Edge with Floodwall
N1 – Riparian Edge
R3 – Evaluate Potential to Raise the Existing Path
R1 – Enhanced River Access

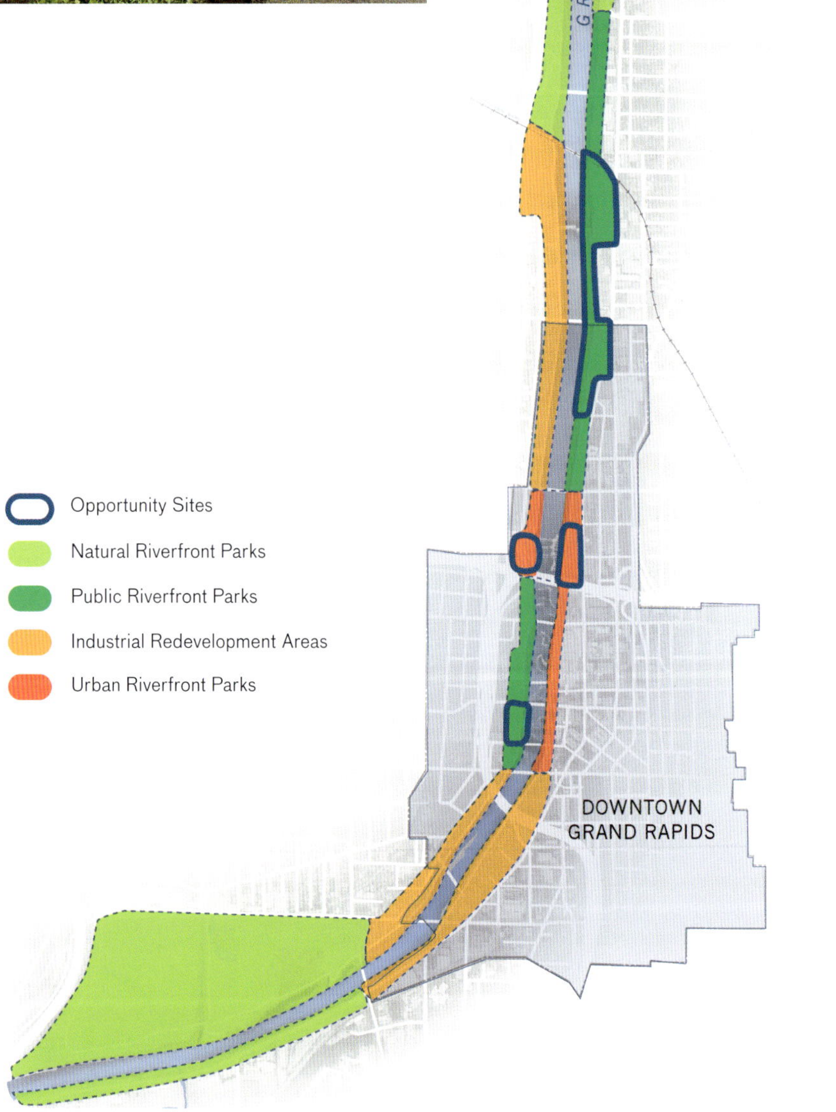

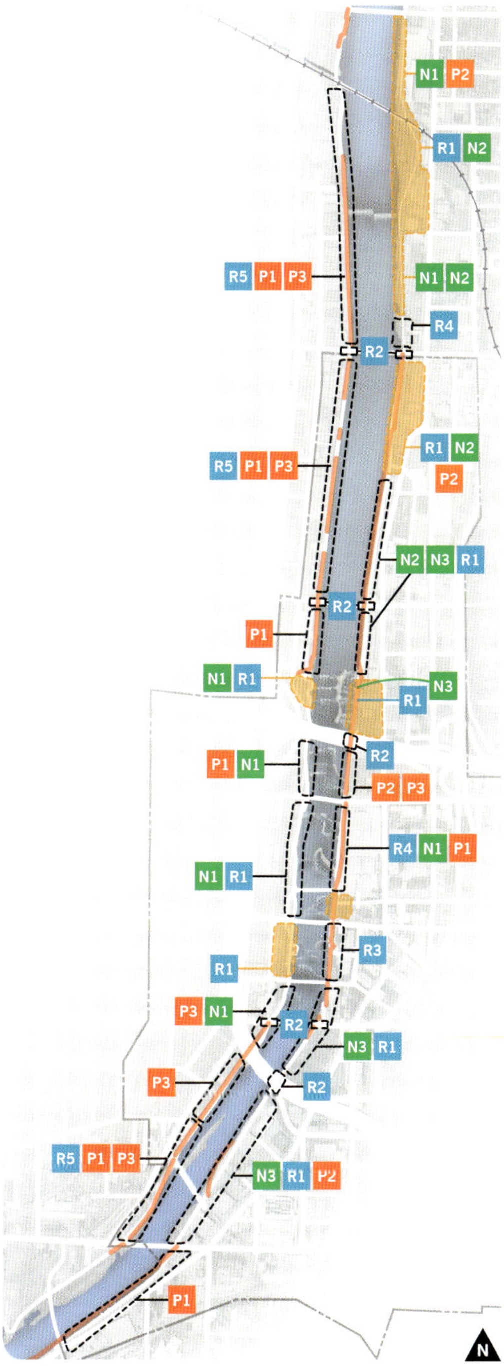


Opportunity Sites and Lyon Square (each have specific design plan recommendations)

Areas that have the following recommended River Edge prototypes:

- N# Naturalized River Edge
- R# River Access
- P# Private Development River Edge

Existing Floodwalls

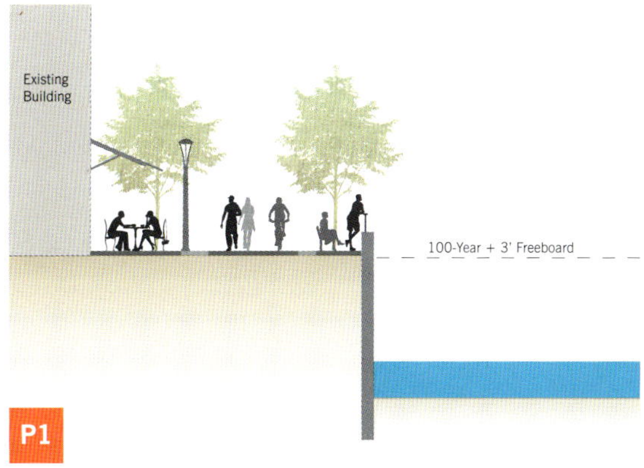


P1

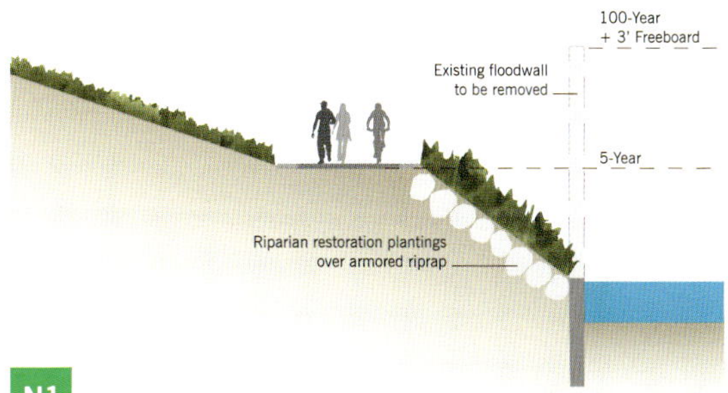


N1

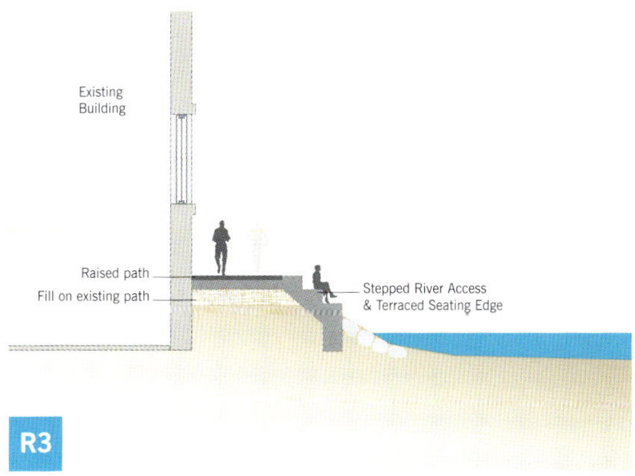


R3

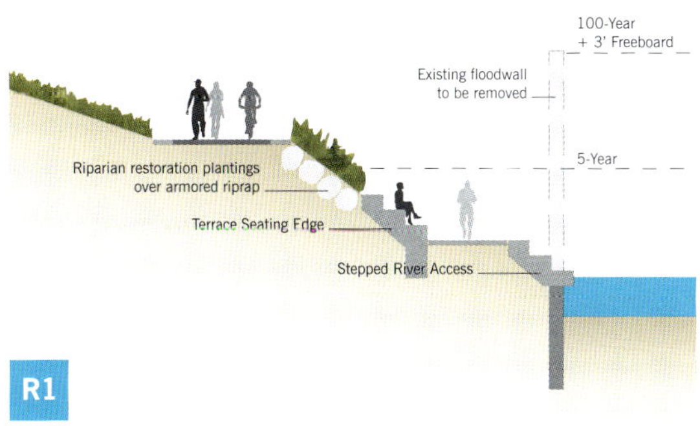


R1

Opposite, top: The Grand Rapids Public Museum plan will reorient the museum to focus on the river and its natural and cultural history through an enhanced environmental education program.

Lower images: Existing neighborhood parks along the river (left) will be modified to restore native plant communities to create more connected habitat and more usable lawns with greater access to the river's edge (right).

Above: Coldbrook Creek historically flowed through this decommissioned water treatment plant to the river. The plan proposes repurposing existing buildings for public use and daylights the culverted creek at the river. Adjacent edges are naturalized to support environmental education programs. Stepped access to the river supports boating access and fishing.

# Los Angeles River Revitalization

Los Angeles, California

**The transformation of the Los Angeles River's concrete-lined channel to restore the river's natural qualities will be possible only through a city-wide transformation of its existing stormwater system to a system based on natural technologies, and reconstruction of the river corridor to integrate natural functions and multiple uses.**

The Los Angeles River Revitalization Master Plan represented a milestone achievement for the City of Los Angeles in its massive scope—to transform thirty-two miles of concrete-lined river into public green space, in the heart of one of America's densest cities—and in its ability to bring together hundreds of diverse stakeholders around a progressive and ambitious revitalization agenda. In the process, Los Angeles made a commitment to restore the river's natural qualities and reconnect park-poor neighborhoods to new parks and enhanced open spaces along the river.

Once a meandering stream up to a half-mile wide and lined with groves of native trees and lush meadows, the Los Angeles River was transformed into a narrow 100- to 200-foot-wide concrete-lined and trapezoid-shaped channel after a series of devastating floods in the 1930s. The city grew rapidly along the river's channelized banks, and dramatic increases in stormwater runoff brought a toxic mix of nitrogen, bacteria, trash, and metals, significantly degrading the river's water quality. Constrained by rail lines, roadways, warehouses, industrial uses, and neighborhoods, the river was all but invisible and largely inaccessible, having been fenced off for safety reasons. The revitalization plan seeks to reclaim over 750 acres along the concrete-lined river channel for multiple-benefit uses, including restored riparian habitat, stormwater runoff treatment and flood risk reduction, potential supplement to the city's water supply, a new interconnected network of parks and trails, and river-oriented redevelopment. The long-range goals are to support birds and mammals and to restore fish passages and pools for steelhead trout habitat, as well as to safely bring people to the river's edge.

The expansive urban redevelopment of the Los Angeles River requires ongoing coordination with the U.S. Army Corps of Engineers, L.A. County, and the City of L.A., as well as private property owners. Ongoing management of the project is being planned to incorporate a joint powers authority (city and county) and a revitalization corporation that will implement land development and project management. A river foundation has been established that will raise funds to support the projects.

The plan's vision is ultimately about creating value—improving the quality of life for residents, increasing the attractiveness of the city as a place to live and work, and increasing economic prosperity. Core elements of this idea include empowering communities by encouraging participation and consensus-building, creating opportunities for long-term economic reinvestment, and providing an equitable distribution of opportunities to underserved neighborhoods along the river.

Opposite: A section of the Los Angeles River today in Studio City.

Above: Enhancements in Studio City will restore in-stream habitat, improve water quality, and create a continuous recreational corridor.

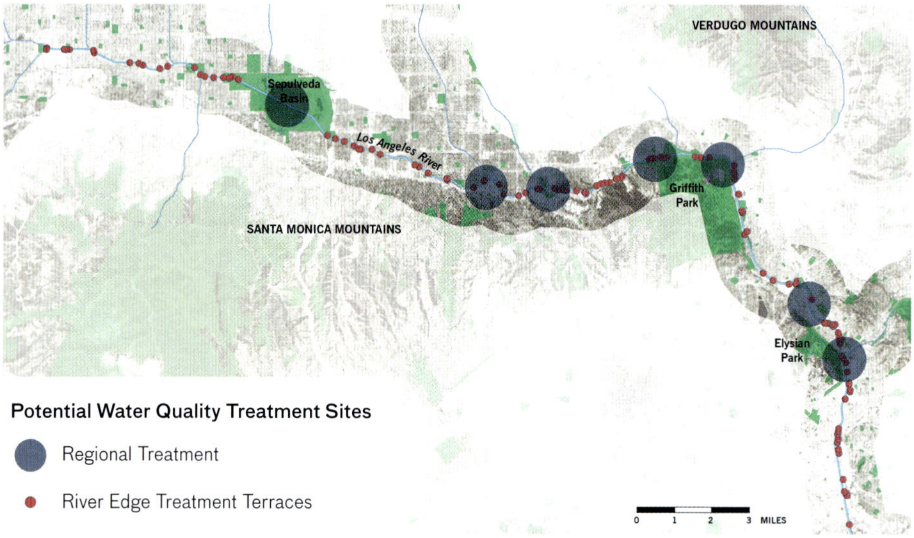


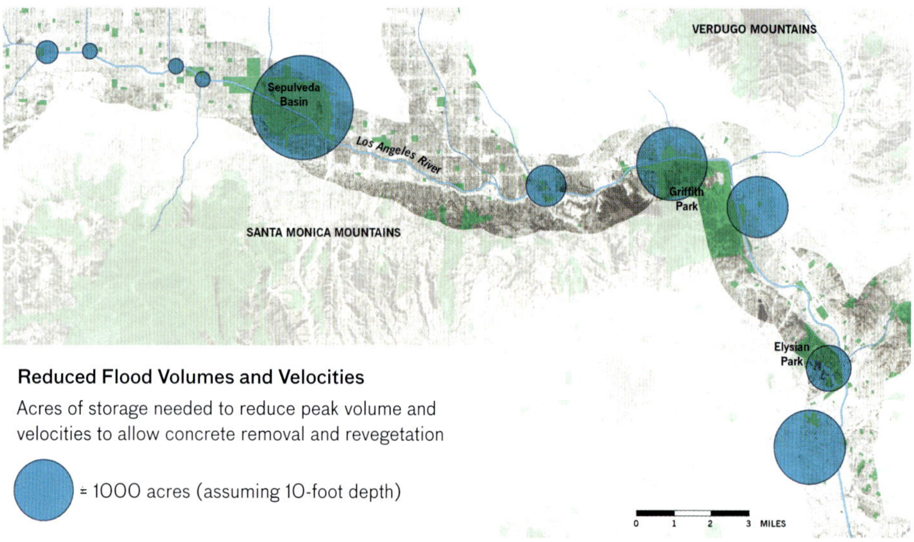


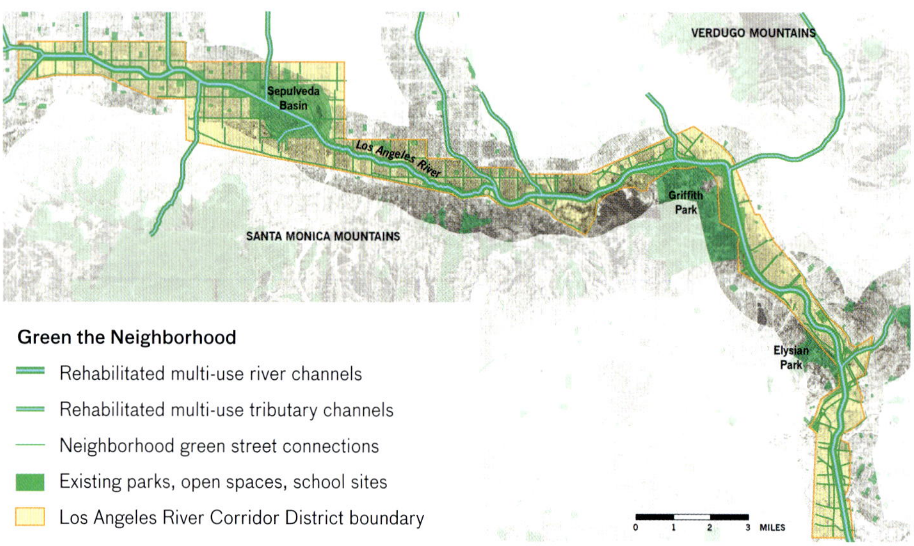


Top map: Several strategies are required to reduce the volume and velocity of flood flows to allow partial removal of the concrete and restoration of the river's natural qualities, and additional stormwater storage in public parks, open spaces, and private developments city-wide will be required to do so.

Treatment of storm runoff from storm sewers and smaller tributary streams will be achieved using natural technologies in public rights-of-way and other underused parcels along the river.

Middle map: Each circle in the above diagram is a scaled representation of the number of acres required to reduce river flow velocities to allow for partial removal of the channel and to support the maintenance and reestablishment of vegetation.

Bottom map: A continuous river greenway would serve as the city's "green spine," reconnecting neighborhoods to the river and linking to a system of "green streets" leading to new parks and open spaces.

Top map: The multiple values of a restored river will promote the redevelopment of dozens of underused areas identified in the plan.

Bottom map: Restoration of the river's natural qualities, combined with restoration of the river's tributaries, will reconnect to mountain habitats that have become isolated because of urbanization.

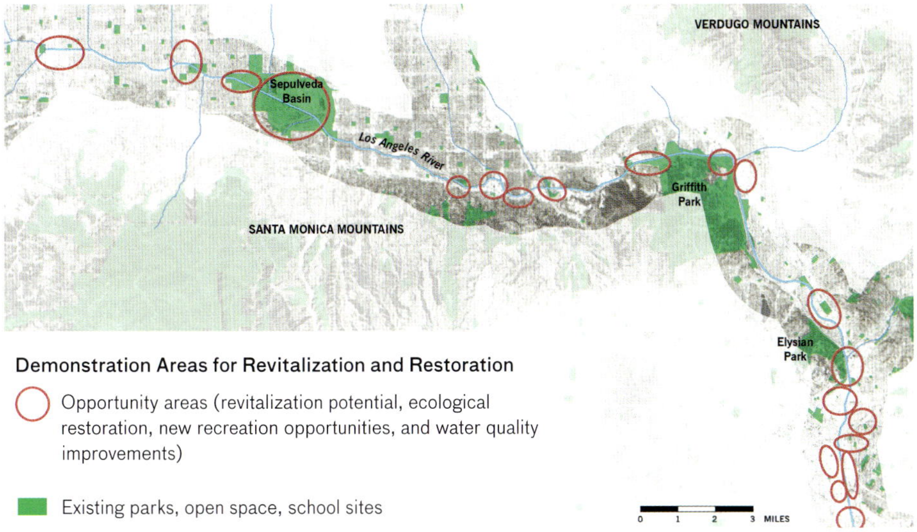


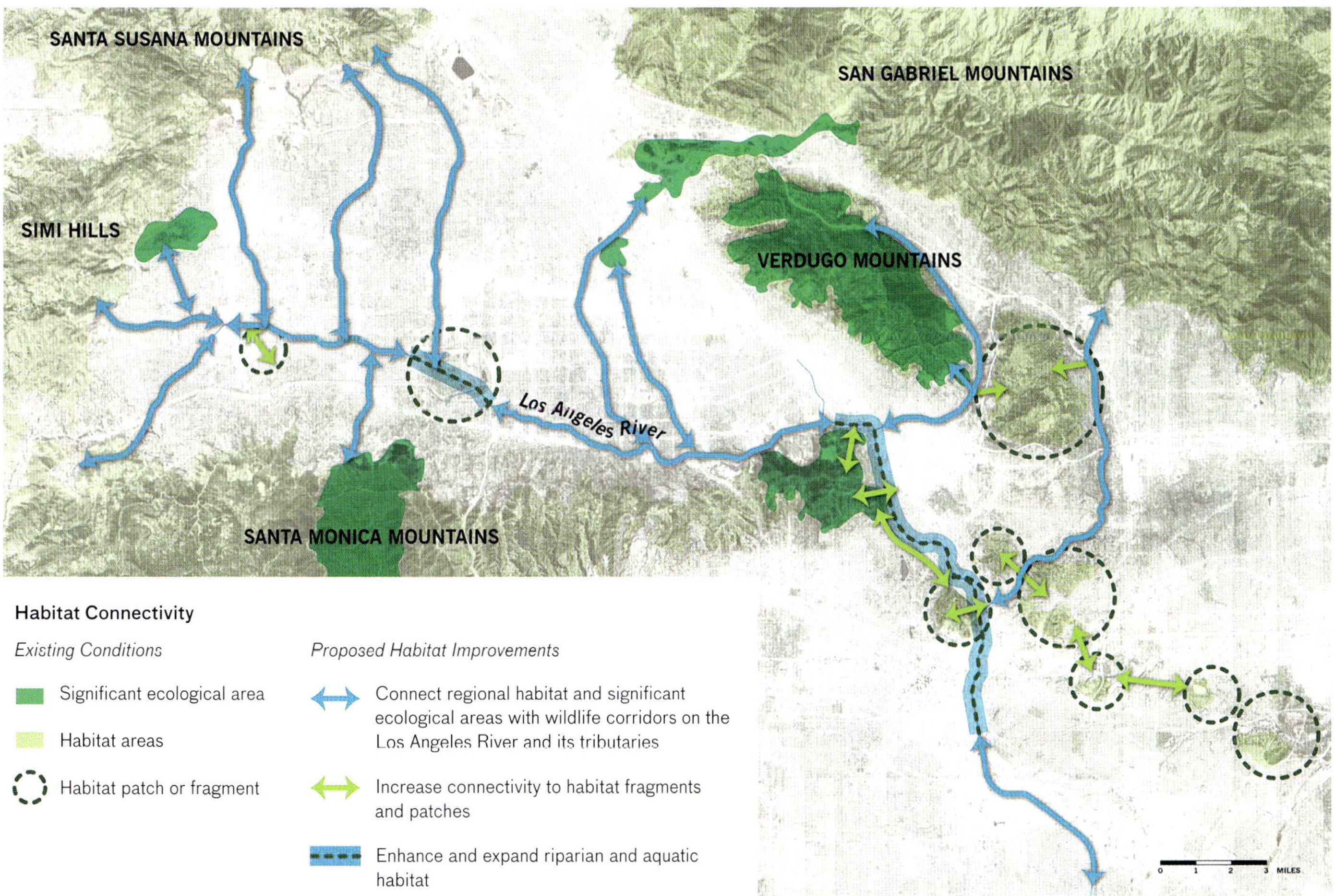

Left: A typical upper section of the Los Angeles River today in the San Fernando Valley.

Above: Near-term recreational enhancements will incorporate pedestrian trails and enhanced plantings along the existing channel before additional flood storage has been created that allow removal of portions of the concrete lining.

Opposite, top: The channel will be reconstructed to restore instream habitat and river access once flood volumes have been reduced.

Taylor rail yard today (above left) and in the future as a large park and natural area (above right). Large, underused sites such as Taylor rail yard or highway rights-of-way along the river will be repurposed as multifunctional stormwater treatment and storage and open-space facilities.

Above: Side channel diversions from the river are proposed to create opportunities for water sports.

Opposite, top: New and expanded parks, improved neighborhood access, and infill development are proposed to revitalize existing neighborhoods.

Opposite, bottom: The plan recommends storing flood flows outside of the river channel and treating stormwater discharges from large storm drains and tributary streams in existing highway rights-of-way and adjacent underused lands.

## Part III

# What We've Learned

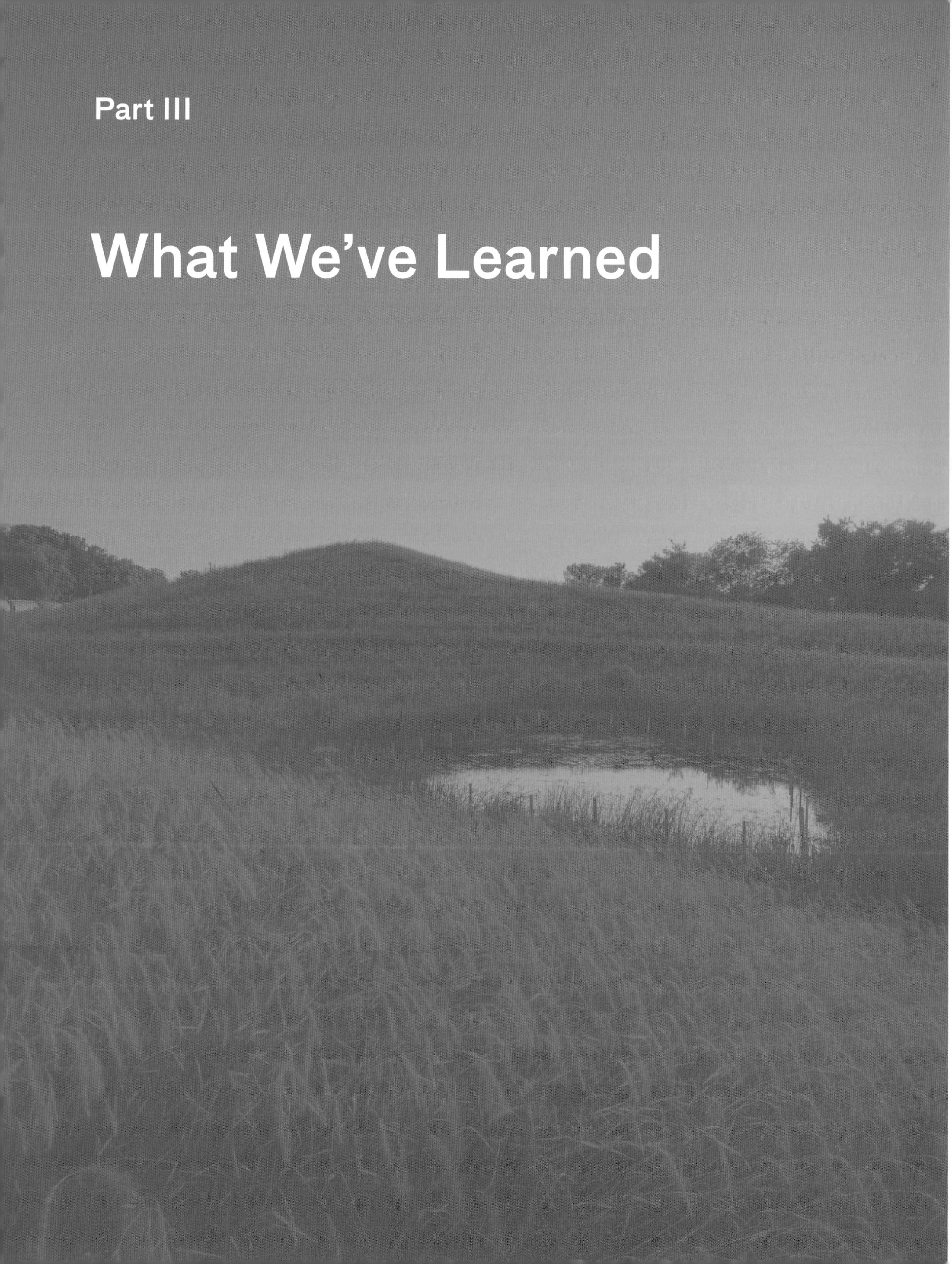

Part III shares what we have learned after observing our projects and built work over a period of many years, in the hope that our insights will help in the design of more effective stormwater control systems. Perhaps the most important lesson is that design professions play only a small part of an extensive range of challenges that must be addressed to allow for broader implementation of natural technologies. Although the role of the landscape architect may be small, it is critical to seeing the big picture. Through the profession's involvement we can integrate multiple values and functions into the city's infrastructure and communicate those values to affected communities.

Part III includes the following three sections:

### Incentivizing District-Scale Stormwater Control Systems

*Design professionals must demonstrate responsible alternatives to existing systems.* This section describes a market-driven scenario for an urban stormwater system at a neighborhood scale that integrates gray infrastructure and natural technologies and describes the civic and financial benefits that are possible through an integrated approach.

### Barriers to Implementation of Natural Technologies

*Multiple barriers limit project scale and how stormwater systems can change.* The second section identifies the public policy, legal and financial barriers, and ingrained professional practices that discourage or prohibit the implementation of larger-scale systems. It describes how entrenched design and maintenance practices can limit innovations in system design, and how better maintenance and management practices could improve performance.

### Looking to the Future

*Green technologies can make cities more resilient, livable, and beautiful, and citizens and designers can be important advocates for change.* The final part describes the importance of the public and practicing professionals as advocates for change, and how public landscapes can be transformed through infrastructure that brings greater value to parks, the public realm, and the natural environment that all cities are part of. It describes how the design professions can build on past projects to implement the next generation of resilient design.

## Incentivizing District-Scale Stormwater Control Systems

Stormwater control systems that employ natural technologies at the scale of a neighborhood, district, or small watershed can be more effective for cleaning urban runoff than individual site, low-impact development (LID) stormwater controls and can provide multiple benefits. New York, Portland, Seattle, Philadelphia, and other cities have more systemic and robust strategies for implementing LID-based stormwater controls incrementally over time. Many large new communities integrate green infrastructure into parks and open-space systems. Malmo, Sweden, and other European and Asian cities are implementing natural technologies at a district or citywide scale, although in the United States, multiple barriers such as legal and financial challenges, for example, have limited this approach.

Concepts that integrate traditional "gray" stormwater infrastructure with expanded "green" LID practices (as shown in the case study described later in this section) are able to move past these barriers and can more easily adapt to the incremental, market-driven growth typical of urban development in the United States. Added benefits include the improved marketability of individual development sites, lower construction and maintenance costs, and improved opportunities for public open space.

### Limitations of Small On-Site LID Stormwater Controls

In an ideal world, individual site LID practices such as rain gardens, green roofs, or other means of biofiltration are the most effective and beneficial means of stormwater control because they treat rainfall where it falls. Although many cities are incrementally implementing LID practices over time, multiple challenges limit their potential. Additionally, individual site LIDs typically lack the civic and open-space potential of larger district or neighborhood scale facilities. In dense urban environments, underground or in-structure treatment technologies such as screening, straining, hydrodynamic, or gravitational separation facilities are often used instead of biofiltration. In controlled conditions, in-structure facilities have proven to perform well; however, they often fail to achieve the levels of performance they are capable of under ideal conditions.

Factors that limit the performance of individual site LID treatment for:

#### Small on-site biofiltration facilities

- poor quality of construction and inappropriate construction details
- lack of, or poor-quality maintenance
- high cost of monitoring multiple small public and private facilities
- at-grade rain gardens may be inappropriate for high-density urban sites

#### Underground or in-structure treatment facilities

- frequent, often specialized requirements for maintenance
- extremely high cost of installation
- complex and costly maintenance requirements

## Benefits of Larger District-Scale Stormwater Systems Using Natural Technologies

Larger-scale, master-planned communities, such as the Lowry Air Force Base or the Stapleton airport redevelopment projects in Denver, are examples of mixed-use communities organized around multifunctional parks and open-space systems that integrate green and gray infrastructure to manage and treat stormwater for the entire community, rather than management on individual properties. Many cities are incorporating district-scale natural technologies in new, higher-density urban districts. For example, green and gray technologies have been successfully integrated into urban parks in the Pearl District at the edge of downtown Portland, Oregon, as part of comprehensive area-wide redevelopment. In an older neighborhood of Minneapolis, Minnesota, the redevelopment of Heritage Park, an outdated public housing project to a mixed-density urban neighborhood, is designed around a daylighted creek and parkway and two neighborhood parks that are part of an integrated stormwater system. These district-scale systems have several advantages and challenges when compared to individual site LID practices.

### Advantages of district-scale systems

- More efficient land use for private development, especially in urban settings, through the consolidation of stormwater facilities.
- Integration of stormwater facilities serving multiple sites into multifunctional parks.
- Enhanced private property values, especially adjacent to multifunctional parks and open spaces.
- More control over quality of stormwater facility design and construction.
- Maintenance and management of stormwater facilities by trained personnel.
- Reduced construction, maintenance, and management costs when compared to individual site facilities.

### Challenges for the implementation of district-scale systems

- The incorporation of multifunctional stormwater control systems into larger planned communities is becoming common practice. Although there are multiple European and Asian models of retrofitted systems that integrate components of both green and gray systems in urban areas, in the United States there are limited options for financing infrastructure, and the lack of public-private cooperation and coordination that is a trait of incremental growth typically prohibits the implementation of district-scale systems. Incremental growth and the retrofitting of existing urban stormwater systems with natural technologies at a district scale requires:
- New forms of governance, finance, ownership, and maintenance of infrastructure that integrate public and private maintenance and management responsibilities.
- Successful models for public-private partnerships that jointly plan, fund, construct, own, and maintain stormwater systems.
- Costs that are competitive with conventional systems to incentivize the private sector to participate.

Strategies for financing, implementation, and ownership, and long-term maintenance for transportation systems and other types of infrastructure is becoming common practice in many cities. Similar programs for stormwater systems are being explored by some cities, including Washington, D.C., and Philadelphia, which are developing multiple strategies to promote more robust green and gray systems. These strategies include:

- Formation of new types of quasi-public special districts to finance, construct, own, and operate stormwater facilities through public-private partnerships in lieu of public ownership.
- Incentives to implement natural technologies. Examples include grants, green technologies banking and carbon trading, and reduced, lower-cost plan approval processes.
- New sources of private capital through tax-exempt equities such as Green Bonds, new sources of public capital through nonprofit organizations, or long-term loans similar to programs currently financing low-cost housing.

The Heritage Park neighborhood in Minneapolis, Minnesota, integrates natural technologies into its parks and open-space system. Photo credit: Fred Bonci

## Case Study: Retrofitting District-Scale Stormwater Controls as Part of Redevelopment

The following development scenario describes the multiple advantages of a district-scale green and gray stormwater infrastructure system implemented in response to incremental redevelopment.

Denver's River North (RiNo) District is an approximately six hundred-acre aging industrial area adjacent to downtown Denver that is rapidly transforming into a medium- to high-density, mixed-use urban district. Most of the district's existing stormwater infrastructure is inadequate to serve the types and densities of development anticipated, and chronic shallow flooding occurs in several areas.

Concepts were developed for two stormwater system design scenarios for a hundred-acre redevelopment area within RiNo. The first scenario proposes a conventional piped stormwater system constructed and maintained by the city, with water quality and stormwater detention provided by individual private development as development occurs. The second scenario integrates a piped system for the conveyance of large storms and stormwater detention for up to the ten-year storm event for each city block, including the street and adjacent private parcels on both sides of the street. Natural technologies are used to treat smaller storms to improve water quality in tree lawns in the street rights-of-way and parks along the nearby South Platte River. In this second scenario, the stormwater system would be jointly developed and managed through a partnership of private landowners and the City. Both scenarios meet the City's requirements for ten-year detention, conveyance, and water quality treatment; however, the second scenario, which integrates conventional and natural stormwater management technologies, has multiple benefits including:

- Demonstrated an approximate thirty-five percent reduction in stormwater system construction costs and twenty-four percent reduction in annual maintenance costs.
- Allowed for increased densities on private development parcels.
- Supported the development of natural open space and a linear park along the South Platte River as part of its bio-infiltration system.

*The River North Area Wide Green Infrastructure Study, prepared by Wenk Associates, was funded through U.S. Environmental Protection Agency (EPA) and Metro Denver's Mile High Flood Control District (formerly the Urban Drainage and Flood Control District) grants.

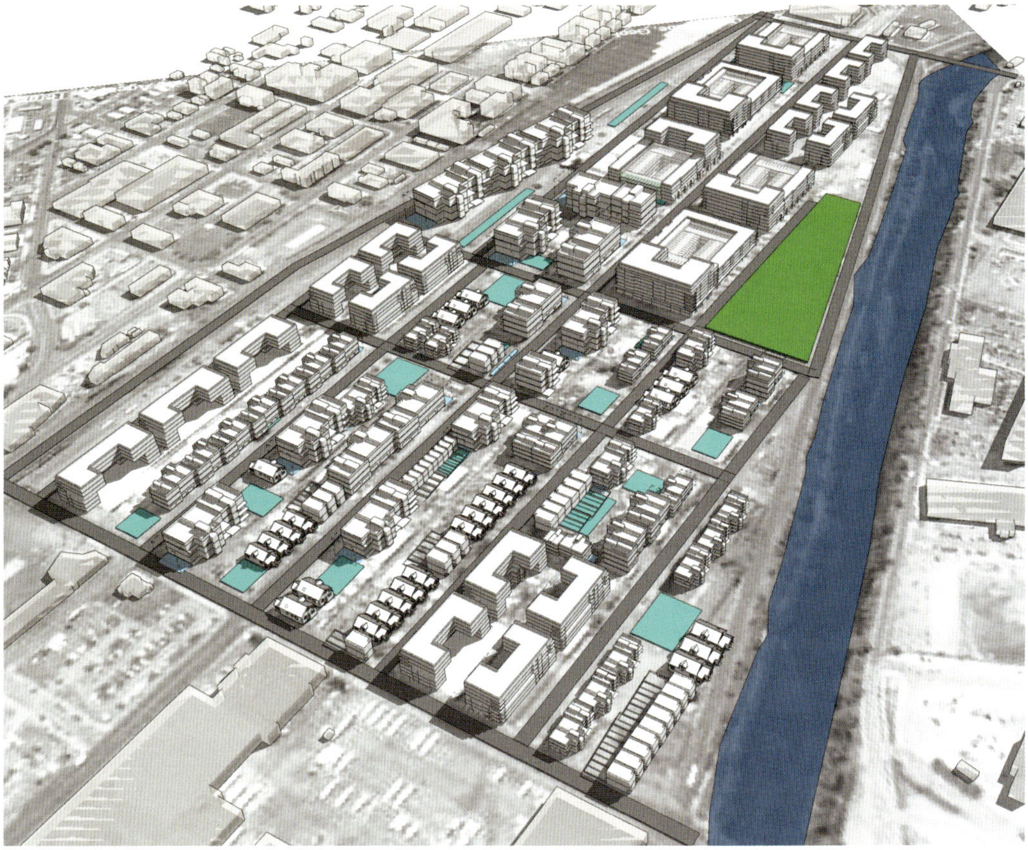

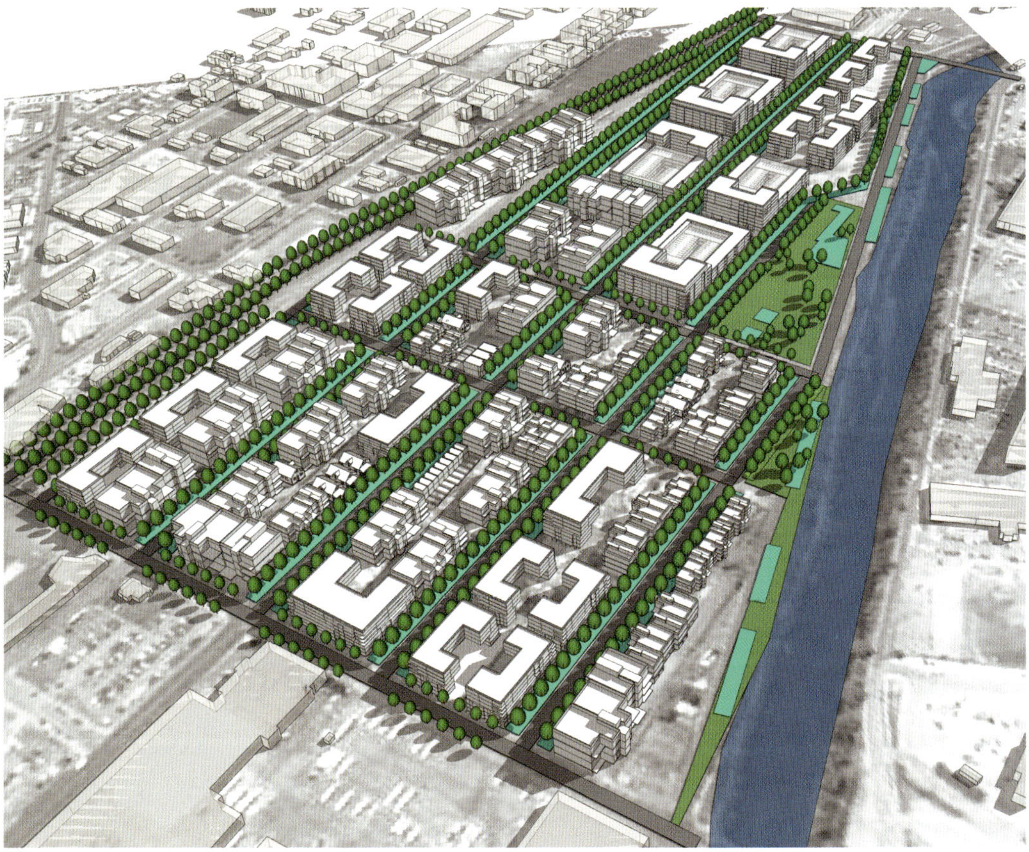

Above: Scenario One: A conventional piped stormwater system with on-site detention and water quality treatment in-structure or by a surface low impact development (LID) facility.

Below: Scenario Two: A conventional and natural technologies stormwater system integrated into the public rights-of-way and a public park and open space along the South Platte River.

The construction and maintenance costs of the second scenario, which integrated stormwater conveyance, water-quality treatment and detention, and enhanced parklands (green areas in the right image), proved to be significantly less expensive than conventional systems described in the first scenario when using street rights-of-way and other public lands.

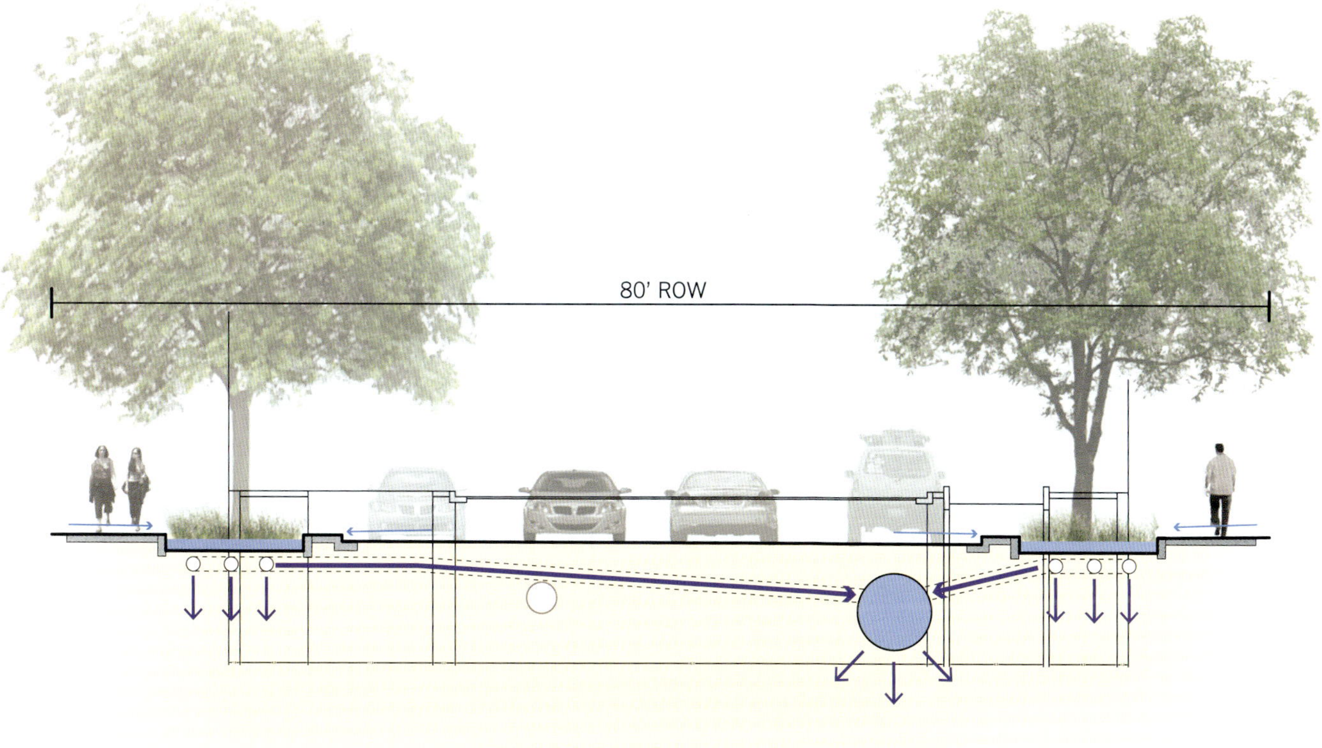

Above: Typical RiNo District street section. Stormwater quality management takes place in the tree lawns, and detention for flood control is under the street in a large storm sewer that stores and infiltrates smaller storms where soils allow. Conveyance and discharge to the river only occurs during very large storm events.

Left: Existing RiNo District. Improvements to the road and storm sewer infrastructure would be necessary under any redevelopment scenario.

# Barriers to Implementation of Natural Technologies

## Managing Risk and Legal Limitations

Change can be hard. And changing long-standing design standards and practices for public infrastructure is especially difficult. Even before design begins, projects are often limited by factors outside of the designer's control. Existing policies and systems, governance, and finance can discourage—if not prohibit—innovative stormwater management approaches. Multiple factors can also limit innovation once design begins. Long-standing design standards and practices, aversion to risk and the potential for legal exposure, lack of coordination, or the reluctance to innovate on the part of design team partners, and other technical challenges can further constrain opportunities to explore new approaches. Following construction, maintenance and management practices required for the proper functioning of natural technologies are often inadequate to maintain a project's proper function. This section will focus on a discussion of barriers to innovation, and ways to minimize the limitations that they impose.

### Water rights in the West—and especially in Colorado—limit options for using rainfall where it falls.

In the West, all surface water and most groundwater resources are owned as private property. Water rights are bought and sold as a commodity. Water that falls on private property under individual ownership is not owned by that private property landowner, and therefore, is not available for the landowner's use. The water is captured in downstream reservoirs and made available for use by the water's owner. Unfortunately, many natural technologies depend on infiltration and bio-uptake of rainfall, which constitutes "beneficial use," and is strictly limited or prohibited under current state water laws in the West.

Unfortunately, at least fifteen percent of the water stored in reservoirs in the upper Colorado River Basin is lost to evaporation annually, which equals five to six times the annual use of a city the size of Denver. In Colorado, water harvesting, or using rainfall where it falls, is illegal with a few minor exceptions. Widespread beneficial use of harvested water, which can include the use of natural technologies to support wetlands and other natural areas, holds tremendous potential to conserve water by effectively using the water currently lost to evaporation. In many Western states, creative ways of trading water rights and other strategies for using rain where it falls should be considered.

### Alternative approaches can present greater challenges and entail greater risks.

Urban streams and rivers and other bodies of water have long been considered hazards. Interaction with any natural environment is not without risk, which can be a significant factor when considering the design of urban waterways (drowning or being swept away, for example). Despite the risk, access to water and its associated natural environment can be among its most important and valuable qualities.

It is important to understand potential risks, applicable design standards and practices to manage risks, and real and perceived hazards. Design must minimize those risks. For example, encouraging river edge access and in-stream recreational use could increase the level of risk for users. An example of limiting risk would be to incorporate multiple options for entering and exiting the river into riverfront designs that allow safe exit from the river. Solutions might include the incorporation of terraced or gently sloping river edge walls or banks, and alcoves or eddies as refuges from fast moving water. Professional judgment, and possibly peer review by a design professional specializing in the specific aspect of the work in question, may be required to limit potential hazards where no standards exist. Full closure may be required during significant storms.

#### Existing standards of care impose limitations.

Although long-standing federal, state, and local policies, building codes and ordinances, and design standards provide guidance for urban development, they are difficult to change and can place significant limits on innovation. Often, standards have been tested through legal precedent, and case law has developed around certain standards of care, which can also discourage innovation. Noncompliance could result in legal exposure and, potentially, actual liability. Project teams may require experts in construction law, zoning and building codes, and other specialties to recommend changes to policies and practices. Designers should identify specific design issues that deviate from standard practices that may require special approval or variances, as early as possible in the design process.

### Overcoming Resistance to New Ideas

#### Anticipate an extended design approval process that could increase project costs.

Many municipalities are unfamiliar with LID practices and nonstandard approaches to stormwater management. Natural technologies and other nonstandard approaches may be prohibited, or additional engineering studies may be required for approval, which can extend the design and approval process. Changes to design standards and typical details can also expose designers to increased liability, so it is important to understand potential risks and address them at the beginning of the design process by working closely with reviewing agencies or informing the client of potential risks, delays, or higher costs.

Many municipalities have implemented innovative policies, standards, and regulations that allow for, or even encourage, more environmentally responsible stormwater management. Separate ordinances for new and infill development—stormwater management integrated into growth policies and design review incentives to speed permitting, among other incentives—have encouraged the use of natural technologies at all scales. Some cities incentivize a reduction in impervious areas through reduced stormwater fees. Referencing standards and practices from more innovative communities can often improve opportunities for success.

### Use examples of successful projects in other cities to educate and advocate for new design approaches.

Designing stormwater facilities for multiple uses is becoming more widely accepted, and standards of care are being established that can promote multifunctional landscapes. For example, *Public Safety Guidance for Urban Stormwater Facilities*, a jointly sponsored publication of multiple professional engineering societies (the American Society of Landscape Architects, American Planning Association, and other organizations), provides design guidance along with appropriate professional judgment and peer review on design approaches that may be outside of existing standards, but that describe protocols for the design of safe facilities. Project precedents—examples of projects that are similar in use and character that illustrate the approach proposed—are also invaluable in communicating new approaches. The most successful precedent projects are from cities of a similar size and in regions of the country with a similar climate and landscape character.

## Limitations Created by Existing Systems of Finance and Governance

### Existing political, legal, financial, and regulatory policies can limit project scope and scale.

District-scale or community-wide transformative infrastructure projects, especially within existing urban areas, are often limited by political, legal, financial, and regulatory policies and practices, rather than a lack of technical knowledge or broad public support. New types of public-private partnerships or new public or quasi-public ownership entities, special districts, and financing described previously, may be required to build and manage projects that cross political, ownership, or other boundaries in the broader interests of the public, and for the benefit of private landowners. New planning tools, such as innovative zoning, may be required.

For example, the Los Angeles River Revitalization Master Plan required that the multiple layers of ownership and management of the U.S. Army Corps of Engineers, Los Angeles County, the City of Los Angeles, and private property owners be managed through a single entity. A key plan recommendation included management of the river through a Joint Powers Authority (City and County), a revitalization corporation that will facilitate land development and project management. A river foundation will raise funds to support the projects. A river improvement overlay district (LA River Improvement Overlay [RIO] District) will apply coordinated design standards and guidelines to new development along the thirty-two miles of river within community planning areas, and facilitate linking watershed and water quality objectives with land-use planning.

### Local planning and building ordinances can limit innovation.

Local planning and building regulations and design standards can often discourage the use of natural technologies. For example, minimum engineering requirements for surface drainage and stormwater piping, which play an important role in how stormwater is managed, may require revision for effective design of biofiltration facilities and other natural technologies. Challenging and updating these standards can slow the progress of a project considerably, with no guarantee of success, and sponsors are often unwilling to risk delaying a project to change standards. For example, Denver's design standards for the TAXI redevelopment project (described in Part 2) initially required that stormwater swales slope to quickly drain away storm runoff. This would have required importing a great deal of earth fill to create the necessary slope for positive drainage, and would limit the potential for biofiltration. After further discussion and analysis, our recommended network of biofiltration swales—which function best with minimal or no slope—were ultimately allowed, and little or no fill material was required. Site development costs were significantly reduced and the effectiveness of infiltration as a means of cleaning storm runoff greatly improved. The following strategies can be used to encourage implementation of green technologies.

## Opportunities for Better Systems

### Incentivize better practices.

The most progressive cities require, but also incentivize, private development to incorporate green technologies into new and existing projects. These incentives, such as reduced development fees and reduced stormwater fees based on a reduction in impervious area, can reduce administrative costs and the time required for approvals, thus encouraging the private sector to incorporate green technologies into their projects.

### Develop market-driven strategies.

*Public-Private Partnerships*—District-scale system construction and maintenance costs can be less than conventional on-site systems, eliminating the responsibility for development and maintenance of individual site stormwater controls. New forms of governance and public finance will be required for broad implementation, especially in existing communities. Transfer of responsibilities to a quasi-public entity allows for cash in lieu of payments for construction and maintenance of the larger system, at a lower cost than on-site improvements. Responsibilities for individual site construction and maintenance are no longer required, which may increase the development potential of individual sites and reduce long-term maintenance costs.

*Revenue-Generating Projects*—In regions where water rights allow, revenue could be generated by storing rainfall as groundwater and using it as a supplement to the existing municipal water supply systems. For example, the City of Los Angeles is proposing to increase the stormwater capture and recharge of urban aquifers as a supplement to the city's domestic water supply and as part of city-wide green infrastructure programs. These are some of the principal objectives of the city's *One Water LA 2040* plan, which proposes to integrate stormwater, potable water supply, and waste disposal into one interconnected system.

## Successful Collaborations Require Shared Knowledge and Mutual Respect

Apart from the small stormwater garden at the former offices of Wenk Associates, the projects described in this book are the result of collaborations between multiple engineering, scientific, and scientific design disciplines working as an integrated team. Contractors are often included in the design process to identify the most efficient means and methods of construction, and for accurate construction costing. Frequently, contractors or construction managers lead the team as an alternative means of project delivery. High-functioning teams share a mutual respect for, and trust in, the abilities of other team members, and have experience with creative problem-solving through collaboration.

The most successful projects are the result of teams that collaborate from the project's beginning to identify potential design approaches that would not seem possible if each discipline worked independently or became involved after major design decisions had been made. Collaboration should be ongoing from concept design through final design. Even when a team shares a common set of goals and a unified vision, it is probable that each discipline will interpret the importance of the details of a project differently, or might identify options that were not obvious in the initial planning and design stages. Because great concepts developed in initial phases can easily be compromised as design progresses, or can be radically changed in the field during construction, it is important to insist on involvement in refining the initial concepts to ensure that the multifunctional and aesthetic potentials of a project are considered from the beginning of the project through all phases of design and construction.

### Develop an in-depth understanding of and respect for the design principles, practices, and technical language of other disciplines.

Engineers, scientists, and ecologists, and other professionals all communicate using a technical language to describe the principles and practices that are particular to their profession. As designers, it is important to have a working knowledge of the technical language of each discipline. A basic knowledge of fluvial and terrestrial geomorphology, hydraulics and hydrology, and the effects of urbanization on stream dynamics, and a general understanding of local natural systems and plant communities is important. All are fundamental to creative and productive team collaborations.

Civil engineers typically bear the primary responsibility for the design of stormwater infrastructure, as they generally focus on the technical design requirements to manage natural forces such as erosion and sedimentation. They manage the flood volumes and channel capacity of urban river streams and related infrastructure, which is also critically important. The technical requirements provide the necessary framework that is the basis for beginning the process of integrating multifunctional components and systems.

Although civil engineers typically support environmentally responsible design approaches, they often focus on the technical design aspects and compliance with design standards. Collaboration with other disciplines, such as landscape architects, can result in exploration of a broader range of esthetic, multiple-use, or nature-based possibilities.

For example, the redevelopment of the Menomonee Valley in Milwaukee required the construction of a primary access boulevard that, because of the flat topography, lacked sufficient slope to drain stormwater by a conventional piped system (and fill was not allowed in the floodplain). Consequently, an elaborate pumping system to discharge storm flows was developed by the engineers. Wenk Associates proposed an alternative road design that recommended "cricketing" (establishing a series of high and low points along the roadway), which would not increase fill in the floodplain, and the development of a series of "green fingers," or biofiltration areas, at low points in the roadway that have little or no slope. The green fingers provide public access and filter stormwater as it flows to the nearby Menomonee River. The client chose the multifunctional, environmentally sound concept because of its lower cost and greater civic and environmental benefits.

Sketch example of one of a series of "green fingers" that would convey and clean stormwater and provide public links to the river's edge. The system would eliminate the need for a piped system.

### Promote interdisciplinary education and practice.

Professional societies, university professional degree programs, and public agencies can do more to promote interdisciplinary collaboration and understanding. They should promote and sponsor the cross-training of professionals in the principles and practices of other professions that are typically involved in the design of multifunctional infrastructure. Professional societies and progressive public agencies can provide necessary research and analysis and advocate for new design standards that limit risk and resistance to change.

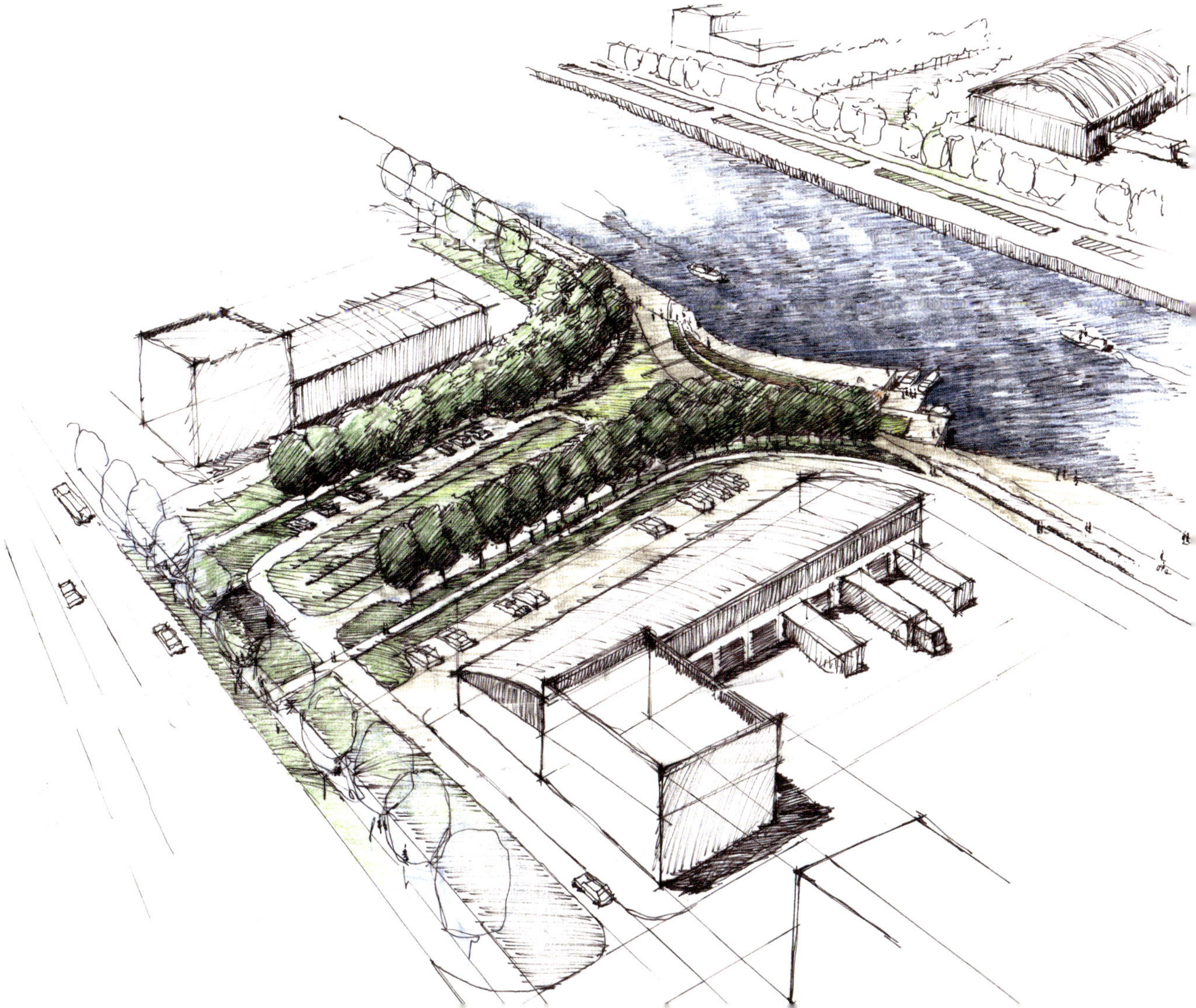

#### Cross-train professionals.

Most engineering and design professions focus on refining the technical skills and knowledge necessary for their respective professional practice through continuing education or specialized seminars. Unfortunately, the knowledge and experience required to fully engage in collaborations with a deep understanding of the principles and practices of other professions is often limited, or professional skills and knowledge that other professions bring to a team are not fully appreciated or understood. Professional certification is needed, like that of the U.S. Green Building Council's LEED (Leadership in Energy and Environmental Design) certification to rate green buildings in the planning and design of green technologies and multifunctional stormwater controls. Certification could be a prerequisite for selecting acceptable team members and could allow for more productive collaborations, and higher-quality projects. For example, Denver's Mile High Flood District conducts a "Stream Academy," an annual series of seminars which includes classroom sessions and field trips for engineers, landscape architects, and other professionals to learn the basic principles and practices related to environmentally responsible stream channel design. Alternatively, universities could develop specialized postgraduate seminars or more advanced specialized training that combines the resources of engineering and design programs to jointly develop curriculums focused on the principles and practices of stream design and urban stormwater management.

#### Recognize the importance of function and performance through professional awards.

Professional awards programs should be expanded to require that the highest level of awards include post-construction evaluation of project performance. Performance criteria should be ranked equal to design and should evaluate the success of natural, social, and functional aspects of the project or system. Specific metrics should be identified, and performance evaluated as a requirement for submission. The submission should include a critique that describes how performance could be improved if metrics are not achieved.

### Project Maintenance as a Design Consideration

Traditional stormwater controls are designed to minimize maintenance by flushing sediment, debris, and other contaminants into urban waterways. Natural technologies are designed to contain debris and treat for contaminants, which requires regular maintenance, including debris and sediment removal, and management of plantings that biologically remove contaminants.
Primary maintenance considerations include the following.

#### Keep it simple. Design robust, redundant systems, and pay attention to the details.

*Waterways* must be designed to anticipate and accommodate the dynamic—and potentially destructive—forces of nature. Considerations include:

- Design for maintenance access by large and small equipment, and minimize the need for labor-intensive hand maintenance. Coordinate with the entity performing maintenance to identify specific needs and requirements.
- Design with redundant (or backup) systems in areas prone to erosion or flood damage. Biotechnical stabilization techniques may fail without additional stabilization, especially if storm events occur shortly after construction. A soil/riprap mix or other armoring as a foundation and supplement to planted areas can provide additional stability necessary for planting establishment.
- Avoid locating trees, other woody plantings, and recreational improvements in areas prone to sediment deposition, to allow for regular sediment removal without damaging the root zones of plantings or recreation improvements.
- Durable construction materials and plantings that can withstand erosive flood flows, sedimentation, and extended periods of drought or inundation by standing water are critical to long-term project viability and success. Agencies that manage urban waterways and stormwater control facilities often require materials with specific requirements for durability, which designers should be aware of at the onset of the project.
- Keep maintenance and management considerations and client capabilities in mind when developing design concepts. Include the client and plan-review agencies in developing plan concepts, and explore the client and review agencies' willingness to develop alternatives to existing standards. Identify the owner's capability for performing maintenance.

**Designers should anticipate maintenance requirements and costs.**
*Natural technologies* must be designed considering context and the owner's maintenance and management capabilities.

- Design biofiltration systems to be self-cleaning to allow for unimpeded conveyance of stormwater runoff, even if regular maintenance (removal of sediment and debris) does not occur, and it no longer functions as a bio-infiltration facility.
- Select plantings considering the anticipated level of maintenance. Unless high levels of skilled maintenance and management will be provided, limit plantings to the most durable and hardy plant species. The poor quality of urban stormwater runoff, and the tendency of aggressive species such as cattails, bulrushes, and willows to overwhelm more diverse or desirable native plantings often limits the type of riparian and wetland plant communities that are successful over the long term without high levels of skilled maintenance and management. Seeding with wetland and riparian grasses and forbs has often proven to be the most durable, maintainable, and cost-effective option.
- Ornamental plantings should be limited to areas where high levels of maintenance can be provided.
- Avoid locating trees, other woody plantings, and recreational equipment or other improvements requiring higher levels of maintenance in areas prone to sediment deposition, to avoid damaging improvements or the root zones of plantings when removing sediment.

## Looking to the Future

Fifty years have passed since Ian McHarg described his vision for the design of a world more in tune with nature, in response to a growing environmental crisis. Implementing his vision is more critical today, given the challenges of global warming and increasingly scarce fresh water supplies. No source of water should be considered a waste, and disposal of rainfall can no longer be considered as responsible management of this valuable resource.

There has been progress. The implementation of massive coastal protection and other large-scale projects demonstrate the local benefits of natural technologies, and incremental implementation of on-site green infrastructure can improve the quality of urban runoff. However, neither approach to managing flood risk or improved water quality is likely to significantly improve the natural function and water quality of urban waterways, unless they can be implemented broadly as standard engineering design practice. A more holistic approach requires better engineering, using natural technologies as a system at a district or watershed scale and use of urban water as a resource for its multiple values and potential. Broad implementation of nature-based systems will require new forms of public policy and finance, public and private partnerships, the active involvement of the public, and new standards for the design of stormwater systems that incorporate green technologies as standard practice, and that are an integral part of the public realm. Then, we can fully enjoy the benefits of healthier rivers and streams, clean water, and more livable cities.

The transformation of urban stormwater systems will profoundly change the urban landscape. New park forms, multifunctional green streets, and a greater diversity of private landscapes can all contribute to the creation of cleaner urban waterways, healthier urban watersheds, and more livable cities. The public and multiple professions will all play a part.

### Communities as Agents of Change

Do not underestimate the potential to leverage the power of the community and visionary thinkers as agents of change to implement new ideas. Some of our most creative, interesting, and environmentally responsible work happened only because of advocacy by strong community individuals and groups that led to support from city leaders. Broad support and political pressure can allow the development of new forms and types of parks and open spaces, streets, and public spaces that are more environmentally responsible and beautiful, enhancing the vibrancy and health of our communities and the natural world.

For example, the community's vision for the Menomonee Valley in Milwaukee led to changes in engineering standards and regulatory review and approvals. It led to the establishment of multiple partnerships that have resulted in the valley's economic revival and the establishment of parks and open spaces that improve the quality of life and health of nearby communities, as well as the natural functions of the Menomonee River.

The long-term success of this revitalized district and its nearby neighborhoods depends on these multiple economic, natural, and recreational functions and values as places for work, gathering, and recreation and renewal, education, and enrichment. Because of these multiple uses, the community has become the steward of their park, making it a safer and more welcoming place. The ultimate success of landscapes that integrate multiple uses and that are a vital part of the city's infrastructure and public open space will depend on the investment of the community in making their park a regular destination for gathering, recreation, and relaxation.

### Creating a Public Realm That Is More Urban, More Natural, and a Center of Community Life

New forms of parks, streets, and public spaces will be developed as a collaborative effort between engineers and urban and park designers. Designers must also work with an array of institutions to develop new types of governance, finance, and maintenance and management that allow us to transform the city at a larger scale, and in ways that are better for the community and the natural environment.

The form and character of urban parks, streets, and landscapes will create a richer and more diverse urban environment, supporting a more vibrant and resilient community that strikes a balance between the multiple functions of critical infrastructure and community gathering, recreation, and leisure use. The natural landscape will be more cultured and will be an important part of the urban landscape. It will function in multiple ways, supporting urban and natural systems, and providing critical functions of stormwater management, and natural settings as places for gathering and respite.

The idea of creating a rich mosaic of functioning urban and natural systems that are an integral part of the city's public and private landscapes is an opportunity to rethink the basic form and function of parks, streets, and other public spaces. New types of parks that integrate access to nature with destinations for community gathering can expand the traditional role of parks and support the natural functions of urban waterways. Linking multifunctional parks into a web of streets and public spaces that integrate multiple modes of transportation, green/gray stormwater infrastructure, and civic and recreational uses provides a framework that mimics the natural flow and function of an undisturbed watershed, accommodates multiple other vital city functions, and becomes the center of the city's public life.

It is our hope that we have played a small part in changing the direction in how we think about working water. The full value of managing urban water resources is possible only through collaboration between multiple science, engineering, and design disciplines. Landscape architects, given their history, skills, training, and ethics, have a key role to play in creating this future.

## Afterword

# Wenk Next

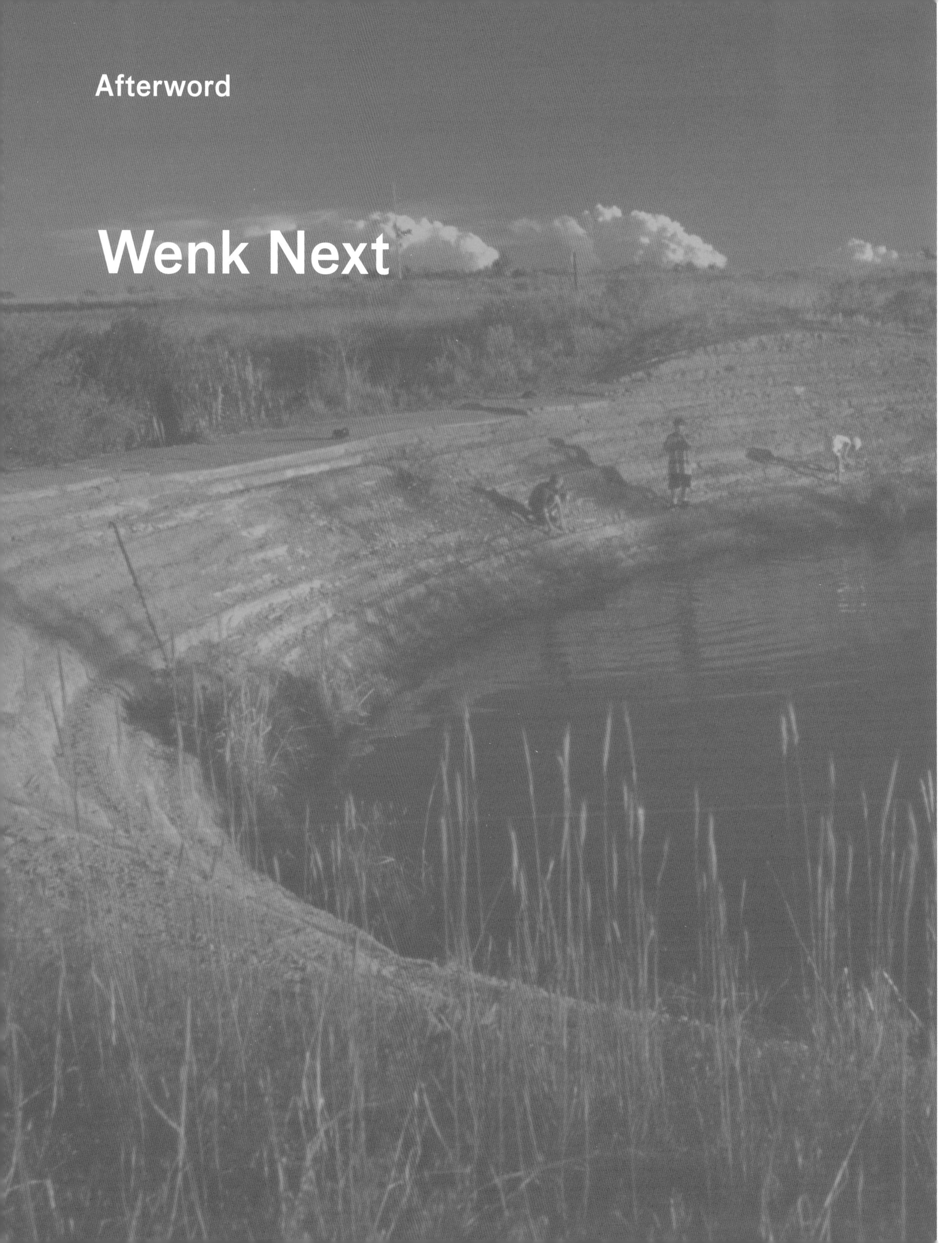

*For two decades, Wenk Associates' principals, Nicole Horst (NH) and Greg Dorolek (GD), have helped build the firm's body of work. They observe what has changed and discuss directions for the firm's work in the future below.*

NH: I joined Wenk Associates in early 2000 and got to participate in construction observation and wetland planting at Northside Park in north Denver. The site included a decommissioned sewage treatment plant and the project established a foundation for a technical understanding of designing with and for water, hydrology, and native plants, as well as the bigger picture of how to transform underutilized spaces into functional and attractive places for people.

GD: I joined the firm in 2002 and was initially drawn to the same project. A *Landscape Architecture Magazine* cover article on Northside Park highlighted a combination of formal design and natural systems-based thinking, then a fairly new concept in the profession. I was also inspired by the thoughtfulness of a selective demolition to expose the remnants of the site's former use, while also repurposing the site for park users and creating a beautiful landscape at the same time.

While these working landscapes are still at the core of our practice, the contexts in which we are working have evolved over the last two decades. Our current sites must be dealt with on multiple levels and present more challenges than they might have twenty years ago. Today, more of our projects are in complex urban areas within former industrial areas that are transitioning into mixed-use urban neighborhoods.

NH: As cities expand, the demands on parks and other public open spaces have grown and their value to the community has increased. Our project sites are more damaged, are becoming more crowded, and will ultimately get more use. As we lead these high-profile public efforts, such as RiNo Park and Promenade, the River Mile, and the Grand River Corridor, we find that the stakes and visibility of the work are higher than ever before.

Working at this larger scale demands that we design parks and open space, urban design, and infrastructure with a comprehensive ecological, social, and economic focus. Within these urban contexts, our approach is far more holistic, and incorporates stormwater management within parks, streets, and public spaces, which minimizes the requirements of individual development sites. We are working to reduce overall infrastructure needs, consolidate maintenance areas, and eliminate the space requirements for stormwater management systems.

GD: Over time, we have seen a transformation in our ability to practice and influence our peer disciplines including architects, engineers, and planners. The role of the landscape architect is becoming broader and more influential. As we lead our recent Denver projects in the RiNo neighborhood and along the River Mile, we are presenting our approach to different city and state agencies, city and county commissioners, regional transportation officials, advocates for pedestrians, bikes, and people tackling different issues of street design. We are building more consensus for what we are doing with more stakeholders, extending support for the idea that our environmental design approach is the right thing to do.

NH: As a profession, our terminology has also evolved over time. Early in our careers we were promoting the benefits of native plants in our landscape, with the advent of LEED. Sustainability was the word of choice that emerged, and now we are discussing the resiliency of our landscapes. Fortunately, the dialogue is more commonplace now, and our clients and peer disciplines understand our work with water, so we spend less time having to convince others of the benefits of stormwater quality, infiltration, and natural landscapes, and more time discussing the experience, function, and aesthetics of the design. We now have common ground.

We are just starting to see the effects of our changing climate on our projects, as storms become more intense and more frequent. In 2015, our Confluence Park project experienced a 5-year storm event that behaved like what was previously mapped as a 100-year event. We are also evaluating the effects of 500-year storms on our projects, rather than just hundred-year storm events. Over two decades of practice, it has been ingrained in our process to understand and build landscapes to meet these increasing challenges of the future. Our most recent work on the Grand River in Grand Rapids, Michigan, is an example of these challenges, where we are reintroducing a more natural riverfront to one that had been channelized for decades with twenty-foot-high concrete walls. We must think in terms of creating river edges that can withstand natural forces and recover for the benefit of the natural environment and the community.

GD: As we look to the future, we know the stakes are higher, but we are excited about meeting new challenges. We know the design and engineering will have to be better, more lasting, and functional. What we have learned over the decades is not just how crucial water is, but also how important infrastructure is as the basic framework of our urban landscapes, and how we as landscape architects can guide and inspire design to make infrastructure more valuable, and our cities better places in which to live.

# Working Water Glossary

*Note: This glossary is not intended to provide technical, regulatory, or legal definitions of terms. Instead, it is intended to provide readers with a general understanding of a term or concept. Several of the terms included have been defined in relation to the specific content of this book.*

The definitions of terms included in the glossary have been adapted from multiple sources, including Wikipedia and various stormwater design manuals, including the Mile High Flood District *Urban Storm Drainage Criteria Manual, Volume 3* Glossary, which is a good source for more technically oriented definitions.

**100-Year Flood Event** A 100-year flood is a flood that has a one in 100, or one percent chance of occurring in any given year. The 100-year flood is a widely used standard and regulatory tool to define the physical extent of areas considered to be flood prone along rivers, streams, and coastal areas. The 100-year floodplain is often used by cities and other regulatory agencies to identify the zone along water bodies where the type and extent of development is limited or prohibited, and where flood insurance is often required...

**Aquifer** An underground layer of porous rock, gravel, sand, or silt where water has accumulated over time. Shallow aquifers are typically sustained by a hydraulic connection to surface waters such as rivers, streams, and lakes, and replenished by stream flow or infiltration of precipitation. Deeper aquifers are often the result of water stored through the accumulation of ancient glacial meltwater or other geological or climatological activity.

**Best Management Practice (BMP)** BMPs typically address issues of poor water quality due to increased runoff from impervious surfaces. BMPs include source control practices (non-structural BMPs) and engineered structures or landscapes designed to treat runoff (structural BMPs). Structural BMPs are designed to reduce stormwater volume, peak flows, and pollutants generated by urban development through evapotranspiration, infiltration, or chemical means. They provide temporary storage and treatment of stormwater runoff and typically employ biofiltration, detention, or other physical components as part of the stormwater system. Non-structural BMPs include maintenance and management practices such as street sweeping or reduction in use of landscape fertilizers to control the source of pollutants. BMPs are most effective when used in combination and when selected and designed based on site-specific characteristics.

**Biofiltration (see also Rain/Stormwater Garden, Bioretention)** Biofiltration facilities, often known as rain gardens, are structural BMPs that improve the quality of stormwater runoff by filtration, biological uptake, or chemical processes as precipitation infiltrates through, and is absorbed by plants, soil, or other growth media. Examples include grass swales, filter strips, and areas that slowly release or infiltrate storm runoff.

**Bioretention (see also Biofiltration, Porous Landscape Detention)** Also known as rain gardens, bioretention is a method of stormwater quality treatment that relies on soils and vegetation for reduction of the quantity (volume) of stormwater runoff and removal/retention of stormwater pollutants. Bioretention facilities rely only on storage, infiltration, and evapotranspiration to reduce runoff.

**Channel Stabilization** Urban development, land clearing, wildfires, and other disruptions in a watershed often destabilize streams through stream bed and bank erosion caused by increased volume, duration, and velocity of flow. In addition to mitigation elsewhere in the watershed to reduce flow, channel stabilization through reduction in velocity using jetties, check structures, revetments, structural linings, revegetation, increased channel sinuosity, and other measures may be required to restore stability.

**Clean Water Act** Federal legislation that provides statutory authority for the National Pollutant Discharge Elimination System (NPDES) program and other water quality protection requirements; Public law 92-500; 33 U.S.C. 1251 et seq. Also known as the Federal Water Pollution Control Act. Under the Clean Water Act stormwater requirements, most urban areas must meet requirements of Municipal Separate Storm Sewer System (MS4) permits, and many industries and institutions such as state departments of transportation must also meet NPDES stormwater permit requirements.

**Combined Sewers** Combined sewers are common in older cities where sewage (wastewater) is combined with stormwater runoff in one pipe. Significant problems arise when rainfall events exceed the capacity of combined sewers to treat all flows in sewage treatment plants, requiring raw sewage to be diverted and discharged directly into rivers and streams without treatment.

**Contaminant** See Pollutant.

**Contemporary Integrated Stormwater System** Integrated systems combine the characteristics of traditional piped stormwater systems with a variety of biofiltration and other low impact development practices into a comprehensive system that manages stormwater and daily flow runoff volume to reduce flood risk and improve the quality of urban runoff.

**Conventional (Traditional) Stormwater Systems** Conventional or traditional (gray infrastructure) stormwater systems rely primarily on subsurface piping and surface channels to convey stormwater directly to a point of discharge into a river or stream. Conventional systems may also include surface or sub-surface detention ponds to reduce the flow rate, thereby increasing the capacity of systems. Conventional systems typically do not include facilities to improve water quality.

**Culvert** A short, closed (covered) conduit or pipe that passes stormwater runoff under an embankment, usually a roadway.

**Daylighted/Daylighting (as in daylighting a river or stream)** Daylighting an urban waterway includes the excavation and rehabilitation of an existing buried urban waterway as a naturalized surface stream channel. Typically, the daylighted channel retains its function as a conveyance in the city's stormwater control system.

**Deposition** Deposition refers to the accumulation of sediment in rivers, streams, and stormwater control facilities such as detention ponds.

**Destabilization/Waterway Destabilization** See Channel Stabilization.

**District/District-Scale** A district is an urbanized area typically bounded by major streets or natural boundaries that ideally would generally correspond with a small watershed or sewershed. Districts can also be defined by named neighborhoods with a well-defined physical or cultural identity, character, or physical boundaries.

**Drainage/Drainage Basin (see also Watershed)** A drainage basin is an area of land where surface and subsurface flows of water collect and drain into a common outlet, such as a river or other body of water. Small drainage basins connect into larger drainage basins at lower elevations. Drainage basins can also be described with the terms catchment area, catchment basin, drainage area, river basin, or watershed.

**Erosion** The process of land wearing away due to actions of wind, water, or human activity. Often the eroded debris (silt or sediment) becomes a pollutant via stormwater runoff. Erosion occurs naturally but can be intensified by land clearing activities such as farming, development, road building, and timber harvesting that remove established vegetation.

**Evapotranspiration** Evaporation accounts for the movement of water to the air from the soil, vegetation, and water bodies. Transpiration includes the movement of water within a plant and the subsequent loss of water as vapor. Evapotranspiration is the sum of evaporation and plant transpiration from the earth and water bodies to the atmosphere.

**Facilities/Stormwater Facilities** A commonly used engineering term that refers to a stormwater system or specific components of the stormwater system that can include watercourses, constructed channels, storm drains, culverts, and detention/retention facilities that are used for the conveyance and/or storage of stormwater runoff.

**First Flush** The condition, often occurring in storm-sewer discharges, in which a disproportionately high pollutant load is carried in the first portion of rainfall flowing from urbanized areas.

**Flow Rate** The measurement of the volume of water flowing past a given point in a river or stream, typically measured in cubic feet per second (cfs).

**Grass Buffer** A uniformly graded and densely vegetated area of turf grass. This BMP requires sheet flow to promote filtration, infiltration, and settling to reduce runoff pollutants.

**Grass Swale** A densely vegetated surface conveyance channel with low-pitched side slopes that collects and slowly conveys storm runoff and other surface flows. The design of longitudinal slope and cross-section size forces the flow to be slow and shallow, thereby facilitating sedimentation while limiting erosion.

**Green Infrastructure (see also Conventional Stormwater Systems)** A cost-effective, resilient approach to stormwater management using natural and engineered technologies to improve the quality of urban stormwater runoff while providing multiple community benefits.

**Green Roof** A vegetated roof that can be used to treat precipitation and/or provide detention. Green roofs require an engineered structure that can support soils, vegetation, and loads associated with rainfall, snow, people, and equipment. Key components include a waterproof membrane, root barrier, drainage layer, soil/growing medium, irrigation system, and plants.

**Greenway** A linear open space or corridor composed of native vegetation, typically along a river or stream. Greenways can be used to create connected networks of open space that include traditional parks and natural areas.

**Gray Infrastructure (see also Conventional Stormwater Systems)** Includes subsurface piped stormwater systems, surface channels, stormwater detention, and other components that emphasize rapid collection and discharge of urban stormwater into waterways without treatment for point or nonpoint source pollutants.

**Groundwater** The natural movement of rainfall and other precipitation through subsurface soil, rock, and other materials beneath the surface of the land.

**Hydraulics** An applied science using engineering and other sciences required to predict and manage the dynamic physical forces of waterways.

**Hydrologic Cycle/Water Cycle** The natural movement of water in a gaseous, liquid, or solid form on, above, or below the surface of the earth.

**Hydrology** The science addressing the properties, distribution, and circulation of water across the landscape, through the ground, and in the atmosphere.

**Impervious Area** A hard surface area (e.g., parking lot or rooftop) that prevents or retards the entry of water into the soil, thus causing water to run off the surface in greater quantities and at an increased rate of flow.

**Infill Development** The development of vacant lots or enhancement of existing urban properties.

**Infiltration** The process or rate at which water percolates from the land surface into the ground. Infiltration is also a general category of BMPs designed to collect runoff and allow it to flow through the ground for treatment.

**Inlet** An entrance into a ditch, storm sewer, or other waterway.

**Level Spreader** A component of a stormwater system designed to convert concentrated runoff into sheet flow and disperse it uniformly across a slope, thereby preventing/minimizing erosion and promoting infiltration.

**Low Impact Development (LID)** The integration of a site's ecological and environmental goals and requirements into all phases of urban planning and design from the individual residential lot level to the entire watershed. (Other terms commonly used for LIDs include Minimizing Directly Connected Impervious Area and Sustainable Urban Drainage Systems)

**Multifunctional** The design of urban stormwater systems that provide multiple benefits to enhance the natural, recreational, aesthetic, or civic qualities of the urban landscape while also effectively managing stormwater runoff and other minor sources of runoff such as lawn irrigation overspray.

**Natural Technologies** The use of natural processes such as biological or chemical processes, gravity, or other naturally occurring phenomena to convey, treat, or otherwise manage water resources to support natural processes or human activity.

**Non-Point Source (NPS) Pollution** The pollution discharged over a wide land area, not from one specific location. These are forms of diffuse pollution caused by sediment, nutrients, organic, and toxic substances originating from land-use activities and carried to lakes and streams by surface runoff. Non-point source pollution is contamination that occurs when rainwater, snowmelt, or irrigation washes off plowed fields, city streets, or suburban backyards, or other unprotected surfaces. As this runoff moves across the land surface, it picks up soil particles and pollutants, such as nutrients and pesticides.

**Open Space** Land set aside for public or private use within an urbanized area that is not built upon, and that is designed and managed to preserve or enhance natural, recreational, or scenic qualities, or environmentally sensitive areas.

**Outfall** The point where stormwater discharges from a sewer pipe, ditch, or other conveyance to a receiving body of water.

**Permeability** The ability of a material to allow the passage of water through rocks or soil. More permeable materials such as gravel and sand allow water to move quickly through them, whereas less permeable material such as clay does not allow water to flow freely.

**Point Source Pollutant** Pollutants from a single, identifiable source such as a factory, refinery, or place of business.

**Pollutant (Contaminant)** Dredged spoil, dirt, slurry, solid waste, incinerator residue, sewage, sewage sludge, garbage, trash, chemical waste, biological nutrient, biological material, radioactive material, heat, wrecked or discarded equipment, rock, sand, or any industrial, municipal, or agriculture waste.

**Porous Pavement** Alternatives to conventional asphalt or concrete pavements that utilize a variety of porous media, often supported by a structural matrix, which allow water to percolate though to a sub-base for gradual infiltration.

**Pre-Industrial Technologies** Technologies that were based largely on human-powered methods and animal power and that predated the industrial revolution that began in eighteenth and nineteenth centuries in Great Britain. Industrial technologies relied on innovations such as mechanization and large-scale mass production.

**Rain/Stormwater Garden (see also Bioretention and Biofiltration)** Designed landscapes that capture and treat polluted stormwater runoff. Rain gardens reduce the flow rate, total quantity, and pollutant load of stormwater runoff from impervious urban areas like roofs, driveways, walkways and parking lots, and compacted lawn areas. Rain gardens rely on plants and natural or engineered soil media to detain or retain and infiltrate stormwater and filter pollutants carried by urban runoff. Rain gardens often provide a method to use rainfall to support naturalized or ornamental landscapes.

**Receiving Waters** Receiving waters include waters of the United States, as defined under the Clean Water Act. Receiving waters include surface bodies of water that serve as discharge points for a Storm Water Conveyance System, to water bodies such as creeks, rivers, reservoirs, lakes, lagoons, estuaries, or oceans.

**Rehabilitation** The use of natural systems to restore natural processes and systems to the degree possible in urbanized or other highly disturbed areas where the predevelopment hydrology, physical form, habitat values, or other natural elements of rivers and streams or other water bodies have been significantly disrupted or degraded.

**Resilient** The use of nature and natural systems in the design of communities so that they may recover more quickly after disruptive natural events. Long-term resilience relies heavily on natural regenerative processes.

**Restoration** Human activity that results in the return of an ecosystem to a close approximation of its condition prior to disturbance.

**Retrofit** The creation or modification of a stormwater management practice, usually in a developed area, that improves or combines treatment with existing stormwater infrastructure.

**Riparian Area/Riparian Zone** Vegetated ecosystems along a waterbody that are typically above the normal high-water level. Riparian areas characteristically have a high-water table and are subject to periodic flooding.

**Runoff** Water from rain, melted snow, or irrigation that flows over the land surface.

**Sediment** Soil, sand, and materials washed from land into water, usually after rain. Although sedimentation and sediment transport are a normal part of a healthy stream system, excess sediment as a result of urbanization or land disturbance can destroy fish spawning areas and degrade aquatic and riparian plant and wildlife habitat.

**Sewershed** A sewershed is the area of land where stormwater (or sanitary) sewers flow to a single end point. As with watersheds, sewersheds can be large or small. Many smaller sewersheds lead to larger conveyance pipes or open channels, eventually leading to a receiving water in the case of storm sewers.

**Storm Drain** A slotted opening leading to an underground pipe or an open ditch carrying surface runoff.

**Storm Sewer** An underground system of pipes that carries intercepted surface runoff, street wash, and other drainage, but excludes domestic sewage and industrial wastes except for combined sewers and unauthorized cross-connections between public and private systems.

**Stormwater** Precipitation that evaporates, accumulates, and infiltrates into the soil in natural and/or constructed storage or that flows over the surface of the land as surface runoff.

**Stormwater Controls** Structural stormwater controls are engineered facilities intended to treat stormwater runoff to improve water quality and/or mitigate the effects of increased stormwater runoff peak rate, volume, and velocity due to urbanization.

**Stormwater Detention** The storage and slow release of stormwater from an excavated pond, enclosed depression, or tank. Detention is used for pollutant removal (stormwater quality detention), stormwater storage, and peak flow reduction. Both wet and dry detention methods provide similar functions.

**Stormwater Management** The functions associated with planning, designing, constructing, maintaining, financing, and regulating the facilities (both constructed and natural) that collect, store, control, and/or convey stormwater.

**Surface Conveyance** A means of conducting stormwater runoff above ground rather than in underground pipes, usually involving curb and gutter, concrete V-pan, or channel.

**Surface Water** Water that remains on the surface of the ground including rivers, lakes, reservoirs, streams, wetlands, impoundments, seas, estuaries, etc.

**Sustainable Development** Development that meets the needs of the present without compromising the ability of the future to meet its own needs. Also: Development that maximizes efficiency and functionality of systems while minimizing the consumption of precious resources.

**Traditional Agricultural Irrigation** The diversion of water from existing rivers, streams, lakes, or other water bodies and conveyance by gravity to storage reservoirs or directly to fields for distribution through a surface system by gravity.

**Urban Design** Involves the social, economic, functional, environmental, and aesthetic objectives that result in the plan or structure of a city in whole or in part.

**Water Vapor** The gaseous form of water in the water cycle.

**Watershed (see also Drainage Basin)** That geographical area which drains to a specified point on a water course, usually a confluence of streams or rivers (also known as drainage area, catchment, or river basin).

**Wetlands** Areas that are inundated or saturated by surface or groundwater at a frequency and duration sufficient to support, and that under normal circumstances do support, a prevalence of vegetation typically adapted for life in saturated soil conditions. Wetlands generally include swamps, marshes, bogs, and similar areas.

# Project Credits

*Note: The projects described in this book span multiple phases over multiple years, some over multiple decades. We have made our best effort to recognize all our teaming partners and Wenk staff that were involved in the success of these projects. We apologize for those we might have missed.*

## The Blue Riverwalk

LOCATION: Breckenridge, Colorado
CLIENT: Town of Breckenridge
COMPLETED: 1994
SCALE: 4.75 acres
PROJECT TEAM: Wenk Associates (Lead Consultant) – Landscape Architecture
David Duclos – Design Concept Review
Deb Keammerer – Plant Ecologist
Niels Lundsford Inc. – Landscape Contractor
Stan Miller Inc. – River Restoration Construction Contractor
Tetra Tech Inc. – Stream Restoration Engineering
Robert Tully – Artist
WENK TEAM: Principal: Bill Wenk
Project Manager: David Carpenter
Landscape Architects/Designers: Dean Pearson, Kevin Dunnett, Paul Thomas
RECOGNITION: 2015 Landmark Design, President's Award for Excellence, American Society of Landscape Architects Colorado Chapter
1997 Honor Award for Excellence on the Waterfront, The Waterfront Center
1996 Community Planning Award, *Snow Country Magazine*, National Ski Area Design Awards
1995 Engineering Excellence Honor Award, American Consulting Engineers Council of Colorado

## Burgess Creek Promenade

LOCATION: Steamboat Springs Ski Area Base Village, Colorado
CLIENT: Steamboat Springs Urban Renewal Authority
COMPLETED: 2011
SCALE: 7.2 acres, 1,300 linear feet
PROJECT TEAM: Wenk Associates (Lead Consultant) – Landscape Architecture
Drexel Barrell & Company – Civil Engineering

MEP Engineering – Mechanical/ Electrical Engineering
Noble Erickson Studio – Graphic Design/ Wayfinding Signage
Oddo Engineering – Structural Engineering
HydroSystems*KDI – Irrigation Design
Kracum Resources LLC – Client Liaison
Landmark Consultants – Site Survey
JBCM LLC – Construction Management
Duckels Construction – Construction Contractor

WENK TEAM: Principal: Bill Wenk
Project Managers: Brent Lloyd (Master Plan), Nicole Horst (Design/Construction)
Landscape Architects/Designers: J.C. Culwell, Greg Dorolek, Beth Gulley, Tyrel Sturgeon

OTHER CREDITS: Stan Clauson Associates – Steamboat Springs Mountain Town Sub-Area Plan Update, November 2005

RECOGNITION: 2013 Finalist for Innovation, Urban Land Institute Colorado Impact Awards
2012 Merit Award for Design & People's Choice Award, American Society of Landscape Architects Colorado Chapter

## Confluence Park

LOCATION: Denver, Colorado

CLIENT: City and County of Denver with:
Urban Drainage and Flood Control District
The Greenway Foundation
Colorado Department of Transportation

COMPLETED: Master Plan, 2012
Shoemaker Plaza Reconstruction, 2017

SCALE: Master Plan 7.5 acres, Shoemaker Plaza Reconstruction 1.5 acres

PROJECT TEAM: Wenk Associates (Lead Consultant) – Landscape Architecture
Anderson Mason Dale Architects – Design and Architecture (MP)
Avocet Irrigation Design – Irrigation Design
Clanton & Associates – Lighting Design & Electrical Engineering
ECI Site Construction – Shoemaker Plaza Construction Contractor
Entitlement and Engineering Solutions, Inc. – Civil Engineering, Utilities
ERO Resources Corporation – Environmental
Harris Kocher Smith (HKS) – Survey
HR&A Advisors – Economic Analysis (MP)
KL&A – Structural Engineering (MP)
Jeanne Quinn – Artist
L.T. Engineering Services – Structural Engineering
Merrick-McLaughlin Water Engineers – Civil Engineering,

| | |
|---|---|
| | Hydraulics and Water Course<br>RockSol Consulting Group – Geotechnical Engineering<br>Vigil Land Consultants – Survey (MP)<br>Zoeller Consulting, LLC – Community Involvement (MP) |
| WENK TEAM: | Principal: Bill Wenk<br>Project Managers: Craig Coronato (Master Plan), Nicole Horst (Shoemaker Plaza Design), Tyrel Sturgeon (Shoemaker Plaza Construction)<br>Landscape Architects/Designers: Neil Emick, Laura Culver |
| RECOGNITION: | 2018 Merit Award for Design, American Society of Landscape Architects Colorado Chapter<br>2017 Downtown Denver Award, Downtown Denver Partnership |

## Grand River Corridor

| | |
|---|---|
| LOCATION: | Grand Rapids, Michigan |
| CLIENT TEAM: | City of Grand Rapids, Engineering and Parks & Recreation Departments<br>Downtown Grand Rapids, Inc.<br>Grand Rapids WhiteWater<br>Grand Rapids Public Museum |
| TIMEFRAME: | 2017–2018 |
| SCALE: | 7.5-mile corridor |
| PROJECT TEAM: | Wenk Associates (Lead Consultant) – River Corridor Planning<br>ETM Associates, LLC – Corridor Maintenance and Management Strategies<br>Fishbeck, Thompson, Carr & Huber, Inc. (FTCH) – River Engineering Concept Analysis<br>Viridis Design Group – Landscape Architecture, Client Liaison<br>Williams & Works – Public Involvement |
| WENK TEAM: | Principals: Nicole Horst, Bill Wenk<br>Project Manager: Megan Jones Shiotani<br>Landscape Architects/Designers: Kaitlin Bernal, Kristin Danford, Drew Button |
| RECOGNITION: | 2019 Merit Award for Analysis and Planning, American Society of Landscape Architects Colorado Chapter |

## Los Angeles River Revitalization

| | |
|---|---|
| LOCATION: | Los Angeles, California |
| CLIENT TEAM: | Project Partners Executive Committee Members: City of Los Angeles, County of Los Angeles Department of Public Works, United States Army Corps of Engineers - Los Angeles District |
| COMPLETED: | 2007 |

SCALE: 32-mile corridor

PROJECT TEAM: Tetra Tech (Lead Consultant) – Project Management, Plan Formulation, River Restoration Engineering Feasibility
Asset Strategies – Real Estate Planning
Civitas – Urban Design
Davis Marquez And Associates – Public Outreach
GCG Rose & Kindel – Policy Planning
HNTB – Architectural Design
Mia Lehrer + Associates – Open Space Planning, Complete Streets Concept Design
The Robert Group – Public Outreach
Transportation and Land Use Collaborative – Land Use Policy
Urban Partners – Real Estate Planning
Urban Semillas – Public Outreach
Wenk Associates – River Restoration Concept Planning

WENK TEAM: Principals: Bill Wenk, Jane Kulik
Landscape Architects/Designers: Jesse Clark, Pam Cornelisse, Kristin Danford, Michael Fortunato Perkins

RECOGNITION: 2009 National Honor Award for Analysis and Planning, American Society of Landscape Architects
2008 Honor Award for Urban Design, American Institute of Architects California Council
2007 Honor Award for Regional and Urban Design, American Institute of Architects
2007 President's Award for Excellence in Planning and Urban Design, American Society of Landscape Architects California Chapter
2007 President's Award for Excellence in Planning and Urban Design, American Society of Landscape Architects Colorado Chapter
2007 Honor Award for Excellence in Long Range Plans, The Waterfront Center

## Lowry Parks and Open Space

LOCATION: Denver, Colorado

CLIENT: Lowry Redevelopment Authority

COMPLETED: Master Plan, 1998
Subsequent phases, 2003–2015

SCALE: 230 acres

PROJECT TEAM: *Lowry Parks and Recreation Master Plan:*
Wenk Associates (Lead Consultant) – Site Planning, Landscape Architecture
Bennett Wagner & Grody – Architecture
BRW, Inc. – Traffic Engineering, Drainage
ERO Resources Corporation – Ecologist, Natural Resources

Frasier & Halbe Engineering Company – Civil Engineering, Survey
Goodson & Associates – Geotechnical Engineering
Olin Partnership – Urban Design
Quinby Clune – Graphic Design
Roos Szynskie, Inc. – Electrical, Mechanical Engineering
*Subsequent Phases Design and Construction:*
Wenk Associates (Lead Consultant) – Site Planning, Landscape Architecture
Bennett Wagner & Grody – Architecture
Deb Keammerer – Native Area Revegetation Recommendation
Ground Engineering – Geotechnical Engineering
ERO Resources Corporation – Ecologist, Natural Resources
HydroSystems*KDI – Irrigation
MKK Consulting Engineers – Electrical Engineering
Reizan Structural Engineers, LLC – Structural Engineering
Roos Szynskie, Inc. – Electrical, Mechanical Engineering
Shen Milson & Wilke, Inc. – Audio Systems
URS Corporation – Civil, Structural, Roadway, Water Resources Engineering
Subsequent Phases Contractors
American Civil Constructors, Concrete Express, ECI Construction, Goodland Construction, Richdell Construction, T2 Construction

WENK TEAM: Principals: Bill Wenk, Emilie Ailts (Master Plan only)
Project Managers Master Plan: Greg Batt, Paul Thomas
Project Managers Subsequent Phases: Jesse Clark, Nicole Horst, Graham Smith, Tyrel Sturgeon, Paul Thomas
Landscape Architects/Designers: Walker Christensen, Jesse Clark, Evan Grimm, Ilene Flax, Nicole Horst, Michael Fortunato Perkins, George Pond, Dan Rhodes, Crissy Roe, Mariko Tominaga

RECOGNITION: 2012 Honor Award for Design, Lowry Redevelopment Park and Open Space System, American Society of Landscape Architects Colorado Chapter
2005 Merit Award for Planning and Urban Design, Lowry Redevelopment Parks and Open Space Master Plan, American Society of Landscape Architects Colorado Chapter

## Menomonee River Valley Redevelopment

LOCATION: Milwaukee, Wisconsin

CLIENT: City of Milwaukee, Redevelopment Authority
Wisconsin Department of Natural Resources
Menomonee Valley Partners

COMPLETED: Menomonee River Valley National Design Competition, 2002

| | |
|---|---|
| | Menomonee Valley Community Park, 2012<br>Three Bridges Park, 2015 |
| SCALE: | 133 acres |
| PROJECT TEAM: | *Redevelopment Concept Plan Competition:*<br>Wenk Associates (Lead Consultant) – Site Planning, Landscape Architecture<br>Applied Ecological Services – Restoration Ecologist<br>HNTB, Inc. – Site Infrastructure, River/Floodplain Engineering<br>*Menomonee Valley Community Park:*<br>HNTB, Inc. (Lead Consultant/Joint Venture) – Site Infrastructure<br>CH2M Hill (Lead Consultant/Joint Venture) – Environmental Remediation Planning<br>Applied Ecological Services – Landscape Restoration<br>Edgerton Contractor, Inc. - General Contractor<br>Marek Landscaping, Landscape Contractor<br>Wenk Associates – Concept Design, Landscape Architecture<br>*Three Bridges Park:*<br>Benesch (Lead Consultant) – Civil Engineering, Remediation Planning/ Design<br>Conservation Land Stewardship, LLC – Landscape Contractor<br>Landscape of Places – Landscape Restoration<br>Lunda Construction Company – General Contractor<br>Marek Landscaping – Landscape Restoration Plan<br>Wenk Associates – Concept Design, Landscape Architecture |
| WENK TEAM: | Principals: Bill Wenk, Jane Kulik (Competition only)<br>Project Managers: Greg Dorolek, Billy Gregg<br>Landscape Architects/Designers: Grayson Baur, Adrienne Burton, Kristin Danford, Beth Gulley, Nicole Horst, Crissy Roe, Tyrel Sturgeon |
| RECOGNITION: | 2016 Honor Award for Excellence on the Waterfront, The Waterfront Center<br>2013 Project of the Year (Three Bridges Park), WTS Wisconsin Recognition Award<br>2009 "People's Choice" Award for Brownfield Development, USEPA Conference, New Orleans<br>2009 Phoenix Award for Excellence in Brownfield Redevelopment, USEPA Region 5<br>2009 Grand Prize for Environmental Remediation, Brownfield Renewal Magazine<br>2007 Mayor of Milwaukee's Urban Design Awards<br>2006 Sierra Club Nomination, One of 10 "Best New Development Projects"<br>2003 National Merit Award for Analysis and Planning, American Society of Landscape Architects |

2002 Honor Award for Analysis and Planning and Land Stewardship Award, American Society of Landscape Architects Colorado Chapter
2002 Menomonee River Valley National Design Competition

PUBLICATIONS: Arvidson, Adam Regn. "Most Industrial: Milwaukee Cleans Up the Menomonee Valley but Keeps It Working." *Landscape Architecture Magazine*, April 2016: pp120–135.

## Northside Park

LOCATION: Denver, Colorado
CLIENT: City and County of Denver, Parks and Recreation
COMPLETED: 1999
SCALE: 14 acres
PROJECT TEAM: Wenk Associates (Lead Consultant) – Landscape Architecture
Big R Construction – Demolition Contractor
Goodland Construction – Landscape Construction
HydroSystems – Irrigation Design
J.F. Sato & Associates – Civil Engineering
Semple Brown – Architecture
WENK TEAM: Principal: Bill Wenk
Project Manager: Billy Gregg
Landscape Architects/Designers: Walker Christensen, Kevin Dunnett, Ilene Flax, Meifen Wang
RECOGNITION: 2001 National Merit Award for Design, American Society of Landscape Architects
2001 Phoenix Award for Excellence in Brownfields Redevelopment, Environmental Protection Agency Region 8
1999 Land Stewardship Award and Honor Award for Design, American Society of Landscape Architects Colorado Chapter
PUBLICATIONS: Leccese, Michael. "Enigma in the Garden." *Landscape Architecture Magazine*, May 2001: pp76–83.
McLeod, Virginia. *Detail in Contemporary Landscape Architecture*, pp58–61. Laurence King Publishing; HAR/CDR edition (April 2, 2008).

## The River Mile

LOCATION: Denver, Colorado
CLIENT: Revesco Properties
Kroenke Sports & Entertainment (KSE)
COMPLETED: Ongoing, 2017 - present
SCALE: Development 62 acres, River Corridor 1 mile
PROJECT TEAM: Calibre Engineering (Lead Consultant) – Site, Civil Engineering/Entitlements
Birch Ecology – Restoration Ecology

| | |
|---|---|
| | Black Creek Hydrology – River Morphology<br>Dialog Design – Urban Design<br>Fehr and Peers – Traffic/Transportation Planning<br>Foster Graham – Legal<br>NINE dot ARTS – Visioning<br>Nino & Moore – Geotechnical Engineering<br>Otak – Structural Design, Project Management<br>Ramboll – Environmental Site Assessment, Materials Management<br>S2O Design & Engineering – Whitewater Feature Design<br>Shears Adkins Rockmore – Architecture, Urban Design, Planning<br>Turner Construction – Cost Estimating, Constructability<br>Wenk Associates – Urban, Streetscape, River Corridor Design<br>WSP – Smart Technologies, Sustainability |
| WENK TEAM: | Principals: Greg Dorolek, Nicole Horst, Bill Wenk<br>Project Manager: Tyler Kiggins<br>Landscape Architects/Designers: Alex Arseneau, Drew Button, Eric Pearse, Bryan Peterson, Evelyn Volz, Cale Wagner |
| RECOGNITION: | 2019 Design Award of Distinction, American Institute of Architects Colorado |

## River North Park and Promenade

| | |
|---|---|
| LOCATION: | Denver, Colorado |
| CLIENT: | City and County of Denver, Department of Parks and Recreation |
| COMPLETED: | Park, 2020<br>Promenade, scheduled completion 2021 |
| SCALE: | Park 3.5 acres, Promenade 0.9 miles |
| PROJECT TEAM: | *River North Park:*<br>Wenk Associates (Lead Consultant) – Landscape Architecture<br>BCER Engineering – Lighting Design, Electrical Engineering<br>Entitlement and Engineering Solutions, Inc. – Civil Engineering<br>Laura Curry – Public Involvement<br>L.T. Engineering – Structural engineering<br>HydroSystems*KDI – Irrigation Design<br>Iron Woman Inc. – Construction Contactor<br>Pinyon Environmental, Inc. – Materials Management Plan<br>RockSol Consulting Group – Geotechnical Engineering<br>Tres Birds Workshop – Architecture, Custom Seating, Custom Play Equipment<br>*River North Promenade:*<br>Wenk Associates (Lead Consultant) |

| | |
|---|---|
| | Pedro Barrios & Jaime Molina – Artists<br>Clanton & Associates – Lighting Design, Electrical Engineering<br>ECI Inc. – Construction Contractor<br>HydroSystems*KDI – Irrigation Design<br>Martin/Martin – Civil Engineering<br>Merrick & Company, J.F. Sato & Associates – Site Survey<br>Pinyon Environmental, Inc. – Materials Management Plan<br>RockSol Consulting Group – Geotechnical Engineering<br>Tres Birds Workshop – Elevated Walkway Architecture |
| WENK TEAM: | Principals: Bill Wenk, Nicole Horst, Greg Dorolek<br>Project Manager: Tyrel Sturgeon<br>Landscape Architects/Designers: Bryan Peterson, Laurie Fickling, Eric Pearse, Drew Button |

## Shop Creek

| | |
|---|---|
| LOCATION: | Cherry Creek State Park; Aurora, Colorado |
| CLIENT: | City of Aurora<br>Cherry Creek State Park<br>Cherry Creek Basin Water Quality Authority |
| COMPLETED: | 1989 |
| SCALE: | 0.6 miles |
| PROJECT TEAM: | Muller Engineering, Inc. (Lead Consultant) – Civil Engineering<br>Black & Veatch – Water Quality Design<br>RBI Inc. – Construction Contractor<br>Wenk Associates – Channel/Structure Design Concepts, Revegetation Design |
| WENK TEAM: | Principal: Bill Wenk<br>Landscape Architect: Tina Bishop |
| RECOGNITION: | 2015 Landmark Design, Honor Award and Land Stewardship Designation, American Society of Landscape Architects Colorado Chapter<br>1995 National Merit Award for Design, American Society of Landscape Architects<br>1991 Merit for Design, American Society of Landscape Architects Colorado Chapter |
| PUBLICATIONS: | Campbell, Craig S., and Michael Ogden. *Constructed Wetlands in the Sustainable Landscape.* New York: Wiley, 1999: pp131.<br>Crandell, Gina, and Heidi Landecker. Designed Landscape Forum. Washington, DC: *Spacemaker,* 1998: pp177.<br>Margolis, Liat, and Alexander Robinson. *Living Systems: Innovative Materials and Technologies for Landscape Architecture.* A Basel: Birkhäuser, 2007: pp 68–69.<br>Strutin, Michelle. "Two Parks that Quiet the Storm." *Landscape Architecture Magazine,* October 1991: pp84–87. |

Woodward, Joan. "Chapter 3: Pattern Sources." *Waterstained Landscapes: Seeing and Shaping Regionally Distinctive Places.* Baltimore, MD: Johns Hopkins UP, 2000: pp168–172.

## Taxi Mixed-Use Development

| | |
|---|---|
| LOCATION: | Denver, Colorado |
| CLIENT: | Zepplin Development |
| COMPLETED: | TAXI II, 2008<br>Subsequent phases, ongoing since 2008 |
| SCALE: | TAXI II 6 acres |
| PROJECT TEAM: | Wenk Associates – Landscape Architect<br>Alan Eban Brown Architects – Associate Architect, Owners' Representative<br>David Baker & Partners – Associate Architect, Residential Unit Design<br>Designscapes – Landscape Contractor<br>Harry Teague Architects – Associate Architect<br>Mortenson Construction Company – General Contractor<br>Will Bruder & Partners Ltd. – Associate Architect, Building Massing and Materials<br>York Engineering Services – Civil Engineer |
| WENK TEAM: | Principals: Bill Wenk, Greg Dorolek<br>Project Managers: Greg Dorolek, J.C. Culwell, Tyler Kiggins<br>Landscape Architects/Designers: Beth Gulley, Kelli Schwab |
| RECOGNITION: | 2012 Global Award for Excellence Finalist, Urban Land Institute<br>2009 Land Stewardship Award for Design and Merit Award for Design, American Society of Landscape Architects Colorado Chapter<br>2008 Honor Award for Design, American Institute of Architects Denver Council<br>2007 Mayor's Design Awards (Denver), Design Excellence Award for "Density by Design" |
| PUBLICATIONS: | Wu, Hong, PhD, Assistant Professor, Department of Landscape Architecture, Pennsylvania State University. *Landscape Performance Series Case Study Briefs,* Landscape Architecture Foundation. https://www.landscapeperformance.org/case-study-briefs/taxi-ii. |

## Wenk Office Stormwater Gardens

| | |
|---|---|
| LOCATION: | Denver, Colorado |
| CLIENT: | Wenk Associates |
| COMPLETED: | 1995 |
| SCALE: | 8,000 square feet |
| PROJECT TEAM: | Thomas Varoz Construction |
| WENK TEAM: | Bill Wenk |

# Resources

BOOK REFERENCES

Friedrich, Katja, et al. *"Reservoir Evaporation in the Western United States: Current Science, Challenges, and Future Needs."* Bulletin of the American Meteorological Society Volume 99: Issue 1, pp167–187. journals.ametsoc.org/doi/pdf/10.1175/BAMS-D-15–00224.1.

Jones, J.E., Editor and Chair, Task Committee on Public Safety Considerations for Urban Stormwater Management Facilities. *Public Safety Guidance for Urban Stormwater Facilities.* American Society of Civil Engineers, October 2014. Sponsored by ASCE/Environmental Water Resources Institute (EWRI) (led by the Urban Water Resources Research Council); WEF; National Association of Flood & Stormwater Management Agencies; APWA; AWRA; American Planning Association. ASCE Press: Reston, VA.

Leccese, Michael. "Enigma in the Garden." *Landscape Architecture Magazine,* May 2001: pp76–83.

National Research Council. 2009. *Urban Stormwater Management in the United States.* Washington, DC: The National Academies Press, p83.

McLeod, Virginia. *Detail in Contemporary Landscape Architecture.* Laurence King Publishing; HAR/CDR edition, April 2, 2008: pp58–61.

Wright, Kenneth, P.E., L.S. and Alfredo Valencia Zegarra Ph.D. *Machu Picchu: A Civil Engineering Marvel.* American Society of Civil Engineers, October 2000.

OTHER USEFUL RESOURCES

EPA STORMWATER CALCULATOR

"National Stormwater Calculator." *EPA: United States Environmental Protection Agency.* Accessed at www.epa.gov/water-research/national-stormwater-calculator.
EPA's National Stormwater Calculator is a desktop application that estimates the annual amount of rainwater and frequency of runoff from a specific site anywhere in the United States (including Puerto Rico) modeling estimated performance of green infrastructure stormwater management practices. Estimates are based on local soil conditions, land cover, historic rainfall records, and climate change scenarios.

INTERNATIONAL STORMWATER BEST MANAGEMENT PRACTICES (BMP) DATABASE

International Stormwater BMP Database, developed by Wright Water Engineers, Inc. and Geosyntec Consultants for the Water Environment Research Foundation (WERF), the American Society of Civil Engineers (ASCE)/Environmental and Water Resources Institute (EWRI), the American Public Works Association (APWA), the Federal Highway Administration (FHWA), and U.S. Environmental Protection Agency (EPA). Accessed at www.bmpdatabase.org.
The International Stormwater Best Management Practices (BMP) Database project website features a database of BMP studies, performance analysis results, tools for use in BMP performance studies, monitoring guidance, and other study-related publications.

Clary, Jones, Leisenrig, Hobson, and Strecker. *International Stormwater BMP Database: 2020 Summary Statistics.* The Water Research Foundation, 2020, www.waterrf.org/system/files/resource/2020-11/DRPT-4968_0.pdf.
This report summarizes volumes of technical findings in brief, non-technical language.

MILE HIGH FLOOD DISTRICT (FORMERLY URBAN DRAINAGE FLOOD CONTROL DISTRICT) URBAN STORM DRAINAGE CRITERIA MANUAL, VOLUME 3 – STORMWATER BEST MANAGEMENT PRACTICES

Mile High Flood District (MHFD). November 2010. Urban Storm Drainage Criteria Manual Volume 3 – Stormwater Best Management Practices. Updated and maintained by MHFD. Denver, CO. Accessed at mhfd.org/wp-content/uploads/2021/01/01_USDCM-Volume-3.pdf.
This publication provides guidance for engineers, planners, landscape architects, developers, and Municipal Separate Storm Sewer System (MS4) permit holders in selecting, designing, maintaining, and carrying out BMPs to minimize water quality and quantity impacts from stormwater runoff.

PATHOGENS IN URBAN STORMWATER SYSTEMS

Clary, J., R. Pitt, and B. Steets, eds. 2014. Pathogens in Urban Stormwater Systems. Prepared by the Urban Water Resources Research Council of the Environmental and Water Resources Institute of the American Society of Civil Engineers. Accessible at higherlogicdownload.s3.amazonaws.com/EWRINSTITUTE/c3dac190-e71a-44cc-a432-3ee9a640acfd/UploadedImages/Final%20Pathogens%20Paper%20August%202014%20_MinorRev9-22-14.pdf.
This report serves as a technical resource for local governments working to address elevated fecal indicator bacteria (FIB) in urban areas, particularly with regard to National Pollutant Discharge Elimination System (NPDES) Municipal Separate Storm Sewer System (MS4) permit requirements arising from FIB total maximum daily loads (TMDLs).

## Acknowledgments

It was only through the efforts of many that the work in this book became a reality. Without strong clients that often challenged us to think in new ways to address environmental and societal challenges and that were then willing to take the necessary risks and try new things to implement these projects, they would have never been conceived or built. They are truly my heroes.

Without the firm's talented and dedicated staff and the multiple engineers, scientists, and other specialized disciplines that stepped up and were willing to collaborate and pursue new ways of doing things as well as the extra effort necessary to do things right, the projects that form the core of this book could have never been realized. Although we have made our best attempt to identify and acknowledge individual staff members, consultants, and firms that made significant contributions on each project, we may have failed to include someone as a result of spotty record keeping or gaps in memory. I take full responsibility and apologize for any omissions that may have occurred.

The content and form of the book evolved over time through many discussions with respected colleagues and Wenk Associates staff. Kathleen McCormick jumpstarted the process by interviewing several staff members and suggesting alternative formats for the book. Kenneth Helphand gave critical input throughout the process, as a continuation of discussions that we have had over the decades since I was a student of his in the landscape architecture program at the University of Oregon. His perspective was complemented by the critical review and detailed comments of Ignacio Bunster Ossa who brings a landscape architect's perspective rooted in both professional practice and in the academy. Their critical reviews were invaluable, and I thank them both. John Jones and Ken Wright, practicing professional engineers with Wright Water Engineers, who are responsible for some of the earliest multiple benefit stormwater engineering projects in the country, brought an engineer's perspective to the review process. Ken Wright's seminal work researching the paleo hydrology of the Inca culture also brought important historical context to the evolution of preindustrial urban water infrastructure systems.

I would also like to acknowledge and thank those that contributed their photography to the book, many free of cost. Your images help bring our projects to life for those who cannot visit them in person.

Without the ongoing efforts of Kristin Danford spending untold hours editing, updating graphics, identifying photo credits, and attending to countless details, this book would have never happened. And many thanks to my partners Nicole Horst and Greg Dorolek for allowing me the time and support of the office to complete this project.

To my wife Marlene, thank you for your patience, understanding, and thoughtful comments as the book evolved over time.

Finally, this book would have probably never happened without the encouragement and support of Gordon Goff and the staff of ORO Editions. Kirby Anderson and Jake Anderson have shepherded us through the process as first-time authors. Pablo Mandel has been gracious and accommodating as the book's graphic designer as it came into reality.